MW01629021
TOOLS
FOR
CONQUERING THE
COMMON CORE

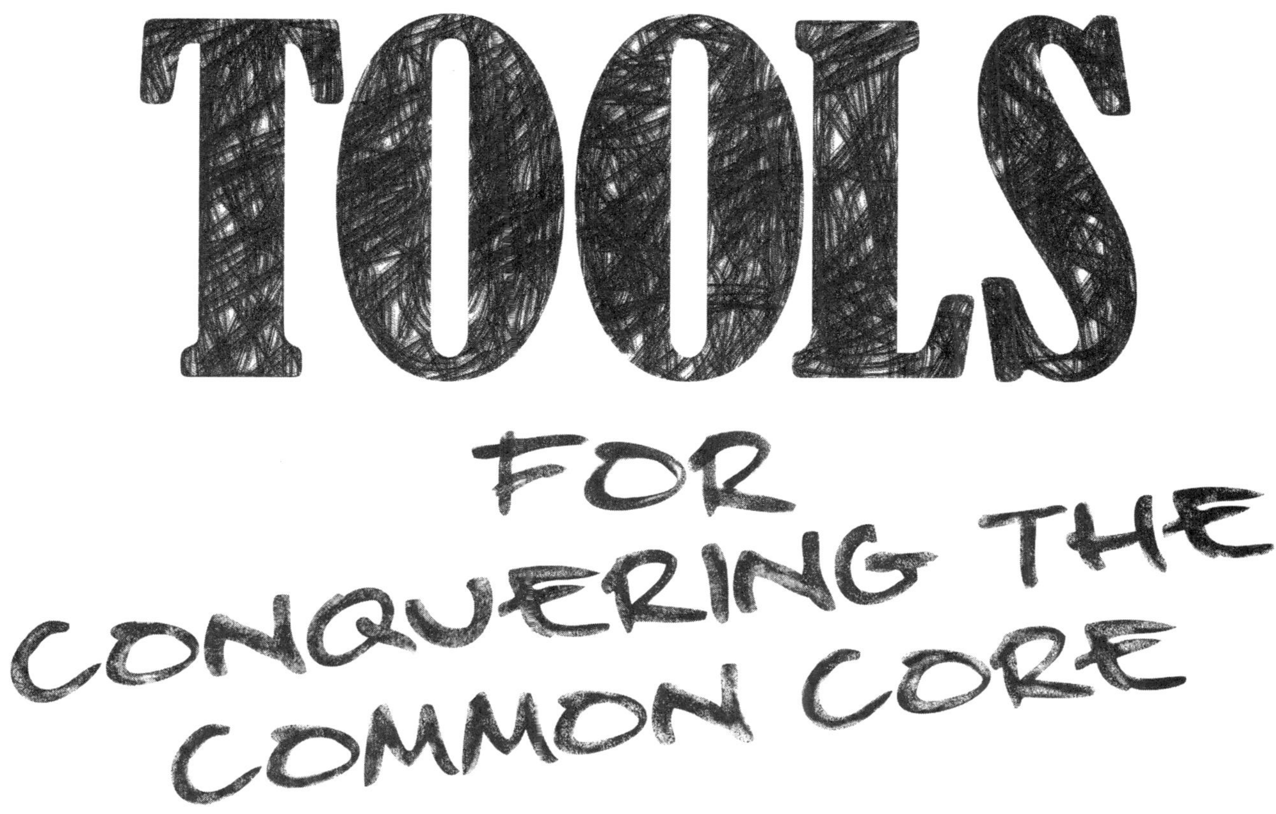

Classroom-Ready Techniques for Targeting the ELA/Literacy Standards

35 tools for developing key skills in

- Reading
- Writing
- Speaking & Listening
- Language

Harvey F. Silver | Abigail L. Boutz

Silver Strong & Associates
Thoughtful Education Press

3 Tice Road, Suite 2
Franklin Lakes, NJ 07417
Phone: 800-962-4432 or 201-652-1155
Fax: 201-652-1127
Website: www.ThoughtfulClassroom.com
Email: questions@thoughtfulclassroom.com

President and Tools Series Developer: Harvey F. Silver
Director of Publishing and Tools Series Editor: Matthew J. Perini
Design and Production Directors: Bethann Carbone & Michael Heil
Proofreader: Christine Hood

All web links in this book are correct as of the publication date below but may have become inactive or otherwise modified since that time. If you notice a deactivated or changed link, please email questions@thoughtfulclassroom.com with the words "Link Update" in the subject line. In your message, please specify the web link, the book title, and the page number on which the link appears.

Printed in the United States of America

Quantity discounts are available. For information, call 800-962-4432.

ISBN: 978-1-58284-203-5
Library of Congress Control Number: 2015933941

22 21 20 19 18 5 6 7 8 9 10

Acknowledgments

First and foremost, we would like to thank Matthew Perini for his thoughtful feedback and assistance throughout the development of this Tools book. We would also like to acknowledge Susan Kreisman's input, particularly her thoughts regarding the direction this book should take.

Others who deserve special thanks include Barbara Heinzman and Ellen Silver for their suggestions regarding the needs of primary-grade educators; Claudia Geocaris, Trisha Layden, and Daniel Moirao for their help in acquiring student work samples; Justin Gilbert for his assistance with permissions and publishing issues; Joyce Jackson for proofreading our standards references; Edward Thomas for assistance with our math examples; Kimberly Wipper and Sarah Stadtlander for their above-and-beyond efforts with regard to images and files; and Paul Boutz for his valuable suggestions and support throughout the writing process.

And finally, we would like to add a note of appreciation for the teachers and administrators who tested our tools in their schools and contributed samples of student work for us to use. In particular, we would like to thank Patricia Acocella, Tracey Germano, and Denise Riccio from Forest Avenue Elementary School in West Babylon, NY; Mary Claire Arena, formerly of Errick Road Elementary School in North Tonawanda, NY; Rae Bastock and Mary Jo Ferguson from Lorain High School Annex in Lorain, OH; Katherine Beery and Max Chernick, formerly of Hinsdale Central High School in Hinsdale, IL; Brenda Donahue, Lisa Murphy, and Cody Pynenberg from Circle Center Grade School in Yorkville, IL; Karen Dooling from East Syracuse Minoa Central School District in East Syracuse, NY; Eleanor Levy and Lyubov Tarasov from Santapogue Elementary School in West Babylon, NY; Christine Miller and Jennifer George from Longfellow Middle School in Lorain, OH; Jennifer Moirao from Kolb Elementary School in Dublin, CA; and the educators and administrators from the West Babylon School District (West Babylon, NY) who were involved in contributing to and supporting the discussion of our tools on their Reflective Pathway blog, especially the blog's moderator, Lisa Granieri.

For copies of the reproducibles
and other downloadable extras noted in the text,
visit **www.ThoughtfulClassroom.com/Tools**.

Contents

Welcome to "Tools for Today's Educators"

The book you're holding in your hands is part of Tools for Today's Educators, a series that we began publishing over a decade ago. We began creating tools—classroom-ready techniques for improving teaching and learning—because the teachers we worked with were asking us for simple but effective solutions for problems they faced in their classrooms. They wanted practical techniques for addressing these problems, not theoretical ones; techniques that they could implement quickly, without a lot of advance planning; and techniques that could be adapted for use in different grade levels and content areas. Most of all, they wanted techniques that would work in real classrooms with real students.

Over the years, we've kept these requests in mind as we developed the various books in our Tools line. We've also continued to ask teachers about the challenges they face in their classrooms so that we can provide them with tools for addressing those challenges. This particular book was inspired by repeated requests for tools that could be used to tackle—and help students meet—the Common Core State Standards for English Language Arts & Literacy in History/Social Studies, Science, and Technical Subjects. Like all of our Tools books, it was designed to promote better teaching, better learning, and student engagement.

Let us know how the tools are working for you and your students. We'd love to hear from you!

Harvey F. Silver
Series Developer

Matthew J. Perini
Series Editor

Introduction

A different kind of Common Core resource

Although the Common Core State Standards were released in 2010, they've become an especially hot topic lately. From cocktail parties to cable news shows, conversations about the Common Core abound. Whether debating the standards' merits, predicting the standards' fate, or discussing standards-based assessment tests, everyone from parents to pundits has something to say.

We've been hearing Common Core conversations in schools as well, but their focus is entirely different. With rigorous new assessment tests now part of the educational landscape, teachers don't have time to discuss the standards' pros and cons; they need to build Common Core skills as quickly as possible, and they need resources that can help them.

This book is one such resource. What distinguishes it from many other Common Core resources is that it is deeply informed by the experiences and needs of classroom educators. We asked teachers and administrators what they wanted (and didn't want) in a Common Core book before we started writing it, and then used what we learned to guide our work.

The result? A collection of thirty-five teacher-friendly techniques (we call them "tools") for developing the reading, writing, speaking and listening, and language skills that are at the heart of the Common Core ELA/Literacy Standards.

Literacy tools for everyone, not just users of the Common Core

We wrote this book to help teachers "conquer the Common Core," but you don't actually have to be using the Common Core State Standards to benefit from using the book. Why? While the book has strong ties to the standards (Common Core connections are noted in every tool), the skills that it targets *aren't* Common Core specific. Rather, they're critical literacy skills that are required by virtually all of today's college and career readiness standards—the kinds of skills that education experts from Harvard University and the Brookings Institution remind us are "a prerequisite to adult success in the twenty-first century" and "essential to young Americans who wish to explore fields as disparate as history, science, and mathematics; to succeed in postsecondary education, whether vocational or academic; to earn a decent living in the knowledge-based globalized labor market; and to participate in a democracy facing complex problems" (Murnane, Sawhill, & Snow, 2012, p. 3).

It is because these literacy skills are so critical for student success, and so integral to multiple disciplines, that all teachers—regardless of what or whom they teach—should be working to develop them. This book enables everyone to pitch in by providing tools that can be used across grade levels and content areas.

To help you understand what the book contains and how to use it effectively, we've summarized some of its key design features in the sections that follow.

Designed to work for busy teachers

We know how busy teachers are, and we structured this book accordingly. Specifically:

We kept things short and simple so that tools could be put into practice quickly. A description of each tool, its benefits, and steps for implementing it can all be found on a single page. Most tools require little or no advance planning, and all have seven steps or fewer.

We formatted each tool so that critical information would be easy to find and use. Every tool contains the same four basic sections (see box below). Large, bold-faced headings let you jump to whichever sections you're interested in, and in whatever order works best for you.

Every Tool Contains the Same Four Basic Sections

1. **What is it?**
   A brief description of the tool and its purpose
2. **What are the benefits?**
   A one-paragraph explanation of the problem/challenge the tool addresses and how the tool enhances student learning
3. **What are the basic steps?**
   A step-by-step description of how to implement the tool in the classroom. For ease of use, each tool includes seven steps or fewer.
4. **How is the tool used in the classroom?**
   A section that provides greater clarity on how the tool can be used and typically includes specific examples from different grade levels and content areas

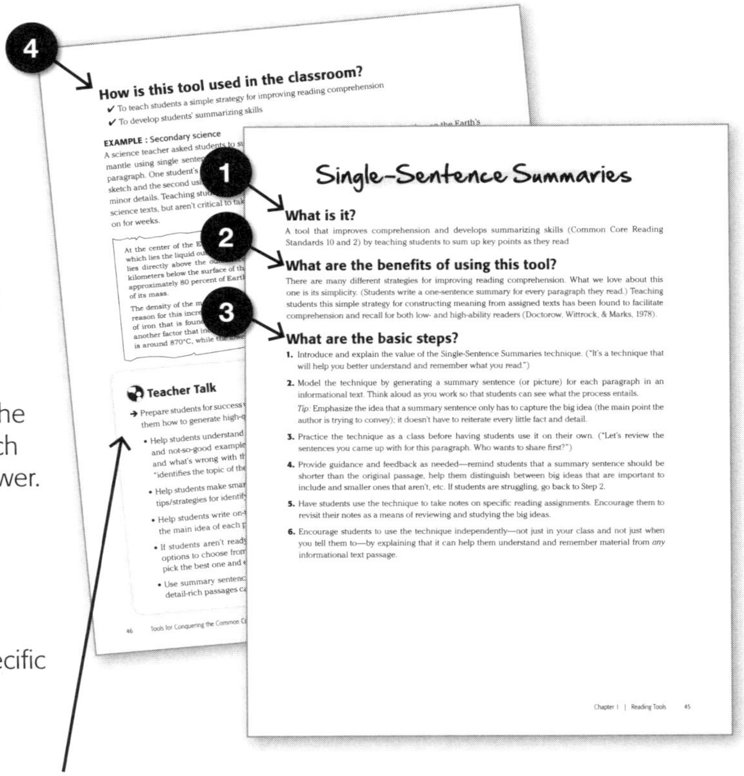

Extras: In addition to the four basic sections, many tools include **Teacher Talk** (tips and suggestions for getting more out of the tool) and **reproducibles**. Copies of the reproducibles and other downloadable extras can be found at www.ThoughtfulClassroom.com/Tools.

Common Core connections are also noted in every tool so you don't have to guess which tools support which standards. Standards are abbreviated as described in our Guide to Common Core Abbreviations (p. 149).

We provided everything you need to get the tools going in your classroom. Besides the essentials, like easy-to-follow steps and ready-to-go reproducibles (available both in the book and on the book's companion website, www.ThoughtfulClassroom.com/Tools), most tools include Teacher Talk—a bonus section filled with teacher tips, simplification suggestions, Common Core connections, and other useful information. Skimming the Teacher Talk section before trying a tool for the first time can help you avoid potential pitfalls and start using the tool like an expert.

We designed the book to be easily searchable, so you don't have to read it from cover to cover. Skim the one-sentence "What is it?" descriptions to find a tool that meets your needs, or use one of the book's search features:

- Use the Table of Contents (p. vii) to search for tools by topic. See Chapter 1 for reading tools, Chapter 2 for writing tools, Chapter 3 for speaking and listening tools, and Chapter 4 for language tools. Don't, however, limit your searches to single chapters since many tools have cross-chapter benefits. A tool from the reading chapter, for example, might also develop critical writing skills.
- Use the chapter introductions (pp 9–10, 51–52, 95–96, and 109–110) to search for tools that target specific skills.
- Use the Index of Standards (p. 145) to see where specific Common Core Standards are mentioned throughout the book.
- Use the Index of Tools (p. 147) to search for tools by name.

Designed to be used flexibly

There's no "right way" to read or use this book. Make it your own by using whichever tools appeal to you in any order you want. Use the tools as written, or modify them as needed to work in your particular classroom with your particular students. Primary-grade teachers or teachers of English language learners, for example, might simplify the language on the reproducible handouts, work through steps as a class, or have students speak or draw their responses rather than writing them. Teachers charged with providing interventions for struggling students might use the tools in small groups rather than with an entire class, or they might offer additional scaffolding.

Designed to be used across grade levels and content areas

The Common Core State Standards call for "instruction in reading, writing, speaking, listening, and language [to] be a shared responsibility within the school" (National Governors Association Center for Best Practices, Council of Chief State School Officers [NGA Center/CCSSO], 2010, p. 4). This book supports that call by providing tools that all teachers—not just English teachers—can use to develop critical literacy skills. Classroom examples show how the tools can be used in different content areas by teachers at the primary, elementary, and secondary levels.

Designed to be used schoolwide

Developing Common Core skills can be challenging. The good news is that you don't have to do it alone. Because this book can be used across grade levels and content areas, you and your colleagues can support each other as you learn, practice, and refine your use of the individual tools. Commit to trying a new tool each month with your professional learning community (PLC). Present a tool at a staff development meeting and make a schoolwide effort to implement it. Or, do what a group of teachers in West Babylon, New York, did and create a blog where teachers can share and learn from each other's experiences with specific tools (http://reflectivepathway.blogspot.com).

The beauty of learning tools collaboratively? Not only will you implement the tools more confidently and successfully, you'll also develop Common Core skills more effectively. Think, for example, how much better students will be at finding textual evidence if it's a skill that everyone in your school has been working to develop, from the earliest grade on up!

Designed to develop the skills that your standards require and your students need

The tools in this book were designed to target skills that the Common Core State Standards and other college and career readiness standards deem critical for student success. Use your standards documents, your standardized test items, and your judgment about the specific skills your students need help with as a guide when determining which tools—or combinations of tools—to focus on. To prepare students for the "support your position with evidence" items that are so prevalent on today's tests, for example, you might first use a tool that trains them to find text-based evidence (e.g., Reading for Meaning), and then use a tool that teaches them how to build text-based evidence into their writing (e.g., As It Says in the Text...).

Designed to be used by administrators as well as teachers

We encourage teachers to assess their students' needs and select tools accordingly. Principals (and other school leaders) can use the book in an analogous way by identifying the skills that teachers need help developing and suggesting specific tools for those teachers to try. This can be done on an individual basis ("When I observed your lesson, I noticed that very few of your students spoke up and shared their ideas. A tool like Speak-Up Stems or Participation Techniques might help you get more students participating") or as part of a schoolwide initiative ("It seems like a lot of you are working to build students' argument-writing skills. Over the next month, let's all commit to trying the argument organizers in the Map It Out tool").

Designed to help students at all achievement levels

While the skills in the Common Core State Standards come naturally to some high-achieving students, most students need to be taught these skills directly. This book enables you to provide this kind of direct instruction by presenting concrete techniques for teaching Common Core literacy skills. The tools-based approach to developing critical literacy skills is one that can enhance achievement in all student populations, but it's especially valuable for average and struggling students. In fact, teachers of English language learners and students identified through the Response to Intervention approach often tell us that their students really benefit from the explicit instruction and structured practice that the tools provide.

Designed to work in real classrooms

The tools in this book were designed to work with real students in real classrooms. To implement the tools successfully, be sure to read the tools carefully, explain them thoroughly, use them regularly, and modify them as needed. Encourage students to apply what they learn by showing them how specific tools (or combinations of tools) can help them tackle assigned tasks more successfully.

Designed to promote learning independence

Prepare your students to become the self-directed learners that the Common Core calls for by teaching them to use the tools, and the skills the tools develop, independently. Introducing the tools using the Five Episodes of Effective Instruction from the Thoughtful Classroom Teacher Effectiveness Framework (Silver Strong & Associates, 2013) is an ideal way to help students master and apply the embedded skills. See the box on p. 7 for an explanation of how to use this approach to teach a tool.

Using the Five Episodes of Effective Instruction to Teach a Tool

Episode 1: Preparing students for new learning

Prepare students for what they're about to learn by explaining the purpose of the tool you're introducing.

Prepare yourself as well by reviewing the tool carefully, walking through the steps in your head, and gathering any necessary materials.

Episode 2: Presenting new learning

Present the tool one step at a time. Explain and model the individual steps (think aloud as you work) so that students understand what they're expected to do.

Episode 3: Deepening and reinforcing learning

Deepen and reinforce students' grasp of what they're expected to do by having them practice using the tool with direct guidance and input from you. (You can do this by working through the tool as a class, or by observing and providing feedback as students use the tool on their own.) Use what you learn from these guided practice sessions to determine whether students are ready to use the tool independently. If they're not, continue presenting and practicing the tool until students are ready.

Episode 4: Applying learning

Ask students to demonstrate and apply what they've learned by assigning a task that requires them to use the tool independently. Assess students' skill level, and provide guidance or additional instruction to anyone who needs it (individual students or the class as a whole). Clarify that students should use the tool whenever it might help them, not just when you tell them to. ("Follow these steps *whenever* you're asked to write an argument—for example, in another class or on a standardized test.") Note that getting students to use a tool independently will require repeated practice and reminders.

Episode 5: Reflecting on and celebrating learning

Encourage students to review, reflect on, and use what they've learned by posing questions like these: What is the purpose of the tool we just used? What are the basic steps? What kind of thinking does the tool build? What kinds of tasks might the tool help you tackle more successfully? Can you think of any other tools that could help you with similar kinds of tasks?

Give yourself time to reflect as well. Think about how the instructional process went and whether you should modify the tool (or the way you presented it) the next time around.

. . .

We hope you enjoy using this book as much as we've enjoyed developing it, and that it empowers both you and your students to conquer the Common Core!

Reading Tools

Frederick Douglass taught that literacy is the path from slavery to freedom. There are many kinds of slavery and many kinds of freedom, but reading is still the path.

—Carl Sagan

Being able to read complex text independently and proficiently is essential for high achievement in college and the workplace and important in numerous life tasks.

—Common Core ELA/Literacy Standards, Appendix A

Reading has often been defined as the "core skill," the single most important key to learning and to success beyond school. But as noted in the Common Core State Standards, there is "a serious gap between many high school seniors' reading ability and the reading requirements they will face after graduation" (NGA Center/CCSSO, 2010, Appendix A, p. 2).

That's the bad news. The good news is that preparing students to tackle the complex texts that they'll encounter on assessment tests, in college, in the workplace, and as citizens in the Information Age, is more than a worthwhile goal; it's a manageable task.

The tools in this chapter were designed to develop the skills that students need to understand and critically evaluate a wide range of texts, both literary and informational. Many of the tools target high-level reading skills that have received increased emphasis in today's college and career readiness standards—skills like supporting conclusions with evidence, evaluating claims and arguments, and analyzing relationships between textual elements. The rest offer fresh takes on skills whose importance has been recognized for years, staples like reading fluently, finding main ideas, and summarizing textual information.

These are the eleven tools that you can use to build these critical reading skills:

1. **AWESOME Summaries** helps students remember the characteristics of a well-crafted summary by converting those characteristics into an acronym.
2. **Choose Your Evidence** uses a simple multiple-choice format to scaffold the skill of supporting a statement with evidence.

3. **Claim Check** teaches students to investigate the validity of claims by gathering and evaluating evidence.
4. **Connection Challenge** trains students to look for and elaborate on connections between ideas, events, and individuals in a text.
5. **Describe First, Compare Second** helps students conduct more focused and detailed comparisons by teaching them to describe the items they're comparing before actually comparing them.
6. **Four for Fluency** presents four easy-to-implement techniques for promoting accurate, expressive, and fluid reading.
7. **Main Idea** guides students through the critical but under-taught process of identifying main ideas.
8. **Reading for Meaning** deepens comprehension and develops critical reading skills, particularly the ability to support a position with textual evidence.
9. **Scavenger Hunt** gets students in the habit of searching texts for specific features, information, and evidence.
10. **Single-Sentence Summaries** helps students get more out of what they read—and hone their summarizing skills—by teaching them to sum up key points as they go.
11. **Structure, Function, Relationships** develops students' ability to analyze structural elements within a text (how these elements function, how they relate to one another, and how they contribute to the text as a whole).

AWESOME Summaries

What is it?

An acronym-based tool that familiarizes students with the characteristics of a well-crafted summary

What are the benefits of using this tool?

Common Core Reading Standard 2 calls for students to craft objective, high-quality summaries of written texts. Before students can write effective summaries, however, they must know what effective summaries look like. This tool helps students acquire that knowledge, both by giving them concrete examples to examine and by turning the critical attributes of an effective summary (adapted from Wormeli, 2005) into an easy-to-remember acronym.

What are the basic steps?

1. Distribute copies of the AWESOME Summary Checklist on p. 13.
2. Explain (and use concrete examples to illustrate) the attributes of a high-quality summary as defined on the checklist. You may want to focus on one or two attributes at a time, particularly with younger students.
3. Help students internalize the attributes of an AWESOME summary by having them use their checklists to evaluate specific examples. Here are some options:
   - Give students examples of high-quality summaries (provide the original passages as well). Help them determine how each example satisfies the criteria in the AWESOME acronym.
   - Give students high-quality and low-quality summaries of the same passage. Help them compare the two summaries using the AWESOME criteria, decide which one is better, and explain why.
4. Test students' grasp of the AWESOME criteria by asking them to revise an existing summary.
   - Give students a short passage, along with a summary of it that fails to meet one or more of the AWESOME criteria. (Create the summary from scratch or use an existing one.)
   - Have students revise the summary using the acronym as a guide and explain their revisions.
   - Use students' responses to decide whether additional instruction is needed before moving on.
5. Challenge students to use what they've learned to summarize a passage that you give them.
6. Remind students to consult the AWESOME criteria both before they begin working (to remind them what they're aiming for) and after they're done (to evaluate their work). Encourage them to revise their summaries as needed based on their evaluations, either on their own or with a partner.
7. Use the AWESOME criteria to give students specific feedback about their completed summaries. For example, "What you've written is 100% *accurate*, but I'm not sure you've included *enough information*. Would someone who hadn't read the passage understand it based on your summary?"

How is this tool used in the classroom?

✔ To help students generate high-quality summaries of information they've seen, read, or heard

✔ To give students concrete criteria for evaluating and improving existing summaries

The AWESOME Summary Checklist can be used to have students write their own summaries or to evaluate and revise existing summaries. The tasks in the examples below reflect these two uses.

EXAMPLE 1: Generating a summary—the focus is on two specific attributes

> Write a summary of this passage. Include *enough information* to capture the essence of the original text, but don't include unnecessary details. Remember that a good summary should contain the *essential ideas only.*

EXAMPLE 2: Evaluating and revising a summary—the focus is on one attribute

> Review the summary of the passage you just read. Identify and remove any unnecessary details so that the summary contains the *essential ideas only.* Be prepared to justify your cuts during an in-class discussion.

EXAMPLE 3: Generating a summary—the focus is on the entire acronym

> Write a summary of the passage we just read. Consult the criteria on the checklist both as you write and after you're done. If you fail to satisfy any of the criteria in your first draft, revise your draft to make it better. Submit the checklist along with your final draft. If you've done your job, every box should be checked off!

EXAMPLE 4: Evaluating and revising a summary—the focus is on the entire acronym

> Pretend that you are the teacher. Give the student who wrote this summary two specific suggestions for improvement. The suggestions you provide can focus on any of the criteria from the acronym. For example, "The sequence of ideas in your summary doesn't match the sequence of ideas in the original. Can you fix that?"

Teacher Talk

➔ In the beginning especially, you may want to have students focus on one or two attributes at a time, as shown in Examples 1 and 2. Once you've introduced (and students have practiced and mastered) all the individual attributes in the AWESOME acronym, you can encourage students to keep the entire acronym in mind as they work (see Examples 3 and 4).

➔ To adapt the tool for use with younger students, you can change the acronym so it covers fewer attributes. For example, teach students to "create summaries that MOM would be proud of" by asking themselves, "Did I retell the **M**ain points or parts? In the right **O**rder? And in **M**y own words?" You can also read passages aloud and have students draw rather than write their summaries.

➔ Since students often have trouble determining which details are essential enough to include and which are minor enough to be eliminated, it's important to model and practice this skill regularly.

Name: Date:

AWESOME Summary Checklist

Consult this checklist *before you begin* so you know what crafting a good summary entails. Check it again *after you finish* to make sure your summary is truly awesome. If it's not, be sure to revise it!

- [ ] Is the information in my summary **A**CCURATE?
- [ ] Has the length of the original material been **W**HITTLED DOWN significantly?
- [ ] Did I include **E**NOUGH INFORMATION to capture the essence of the original material?
- [ ] Is the information in my summary logically organized and **S**EQUENCED?
- [ ] Did I give an **O**BJECTIVE (free from personal opinions) summary of the original material?
- [ ] Did I summarize the original material in **M**Y OWN WORDS?
- [ ] Does my summary contain the **E**SSENTIAL IDEAS ONLY? Did I eliminate unnecessary details?

Choose Your Evidence

What is it?

A tool that supports multiple Common Core Standards by teaching students how to identify and select quality evidence

What are the benefits of using this tool?

According to the authors of the Common Core, college and career ready students must be able to both "use relevant evidence when supporting their own points" and "constructively evaluate others' use of evidence" (NGA Center/CCSSO, 2010, p. 7). In order to do these things, students must have a clear understanding of what constitutes quality evidence. This tool uses a simple multiple-choice framework to help them develop this understanding and practice what they learn.

What are the basic steps?

1. Create a Choose Your Evidence item as follows (use the sample items on pp. 15–16 as models):
- Record a claim (or conclusion) on paper. The claim can be about anything you want—a topic or text you're covering in class, a current event, a school policy, etc.
- Underneath the claim, record four to seven statements. Some of the statements should provide support for the claim; others should relate to the claim (i.e., be about the same general topic), but not provide support for it.

2. Create additional Choose Your Evidence items in the same manner. You'll need some for modeling and group practice (Steps 3–4), and some for students to work on independently (Step 5).

3. Use one or more of the items you created to help students see the difference between information that *supports* a claim and information that *relates to* a claim, but doesn't support it.

Tip: Think aloud so students learn how to go about determining whether a statement does or doesn't support a claim. ("Hmmm... It's true that there are many different kinds of fish, but does this statement support the claim that fish do some really strange things? I don't think so.")

4. Complete and discuss a few more items as a class. Read each claim aloud, and give students time to review the statements that follow it. Have students circle the statements that provide supporting evidence, and then review and discuss their choices.

5. Set aside time for students to practice independently using the rest of the items you created.

6. Review students' work, either as a class or by collecting students' papers. Use what you learn to provide appropriate feedback and determine whether additional modeling/instruction is needed.

How is this tool used in the classroom?

✔ To develop students' ability to select and evaluate evidence

EXAMPLE 1: Primary science

A second-grade teacher designed the item below around an informational text about dolphins (Stewart, 2010). To target Common Core Reading Standard 1 (supporting conclusions with textual evidence), she used specific lines from the text to create her multiple-choice statements.

> INSTRUCTIONS: Circle the details that support the conclusion below. Be ready to explain your choices.
>
> *Dolphins are a lot like people!*
>
> ⓐ Dolphins have lungs and breathe air.
> b) Dolphins get oxygen through a hole on the top of their heads.
> c) Whales and dolphins are very closely related.
> d) More than thirty different kinds of dolphins live on Earth.
> ⓔ Baby dolphins drink milk from their mothers' bodies.
> ⓕ Dolphins like to have fun and play games.

EXAMPLE 2: Secondary history

Here, history students were asked to identify reasons that could be used to support the claim that the United States should end its embargo against Cuba. A companion item (not shown) had them identify reasons that could be used to support the opposing claim.

> INSTRUCTIONS: Circle reasons you could use to support the claim below. Be ready to explain your choices.
>
> *The United States should abandon its embargo against Cuba.*
>
> ⓐ After more than half a century, the embargo has failed to achieve its purpose.
> b) The United States maintains a naval base in Cuba at Guantanamo Bay.
> ⓒ The embargo is estimated to cost the United States $1.2 billion per year in lost exports.
> d) In 2005, Cuba had $2.4 billion in exports, putting it in 114th position out of 226 countries.
> ⓔ It's hypocritical to treat Cuba differently than other countries whose policies we oppose.
> f) An embargo is a government order that restricts commerce or exchange with a specific country.
> g) Cuban citizens need official permission before they can leave or return to their country.

EXAMPLE 3: Secondary health/physical education

> INSTRUCTIONS: Circle the evidence that supports the conclusion below. Be ready to explain your choices.
>
> *Regular physical exercise offers many benefits.*
>
> ⓐ Physical activity can help you maintain a healthy weight.
> b) Many different activities count as exercise, including running, dancing, jumping rope, and playing soccer.
> c) The Department of Health and Human Services recommends strength training at least twice per week.
> d) To get the benefits, aim for a target heart rate of between 50% and 85% of your maximum heart rate.
> ⓔ Exercise can boost your mood by increasing levels of "feel-good" brain chemicals like serotonin.
> ⓕ Regular exercise can reduce your risk for diseases like type 2 diabetes, cancer, and heart disease.

EXAMPLE 4: Elementary mathematics

This example was designed both to test students' grasp of specific mathematical content standards (Common Core 3.G.1.A and 4.G.A.2) and to model the process of justifying a conclusion with evidence (Mathematical Practice Standard 3).

INSTRUCTIONS: Circle the evidence that supports the conclusion below. Be ready to explain your choices.

A square is a parallelogram.

- (a) Squares have four sides.
- b) Rectangles and rhombuses are also parallelograms.
- c) The sides of a square are all the same length.
- (d) The opposite sides of a square are parallel to one another.
- e) You can calculate the perimeter of a square by adding the lengths of its sides.

Teacher Talk

➔ When generating statements in Steps 1–2, you might accidentally (or purposefully) create ones that are debatable rather than black and white. As long as the items are discussed as a class rather than scored for a grade, this kind of ambiguity can actually be beneficial because it promotes discussion and debate, and encourages students to defend their choices with evidence. ("I think the first statement supports the claim because..." or "I think it doesn't because...")

➔ Some students confuse the notion of *providing support* with *being accurate*. (These students will select statements that are factually accurate even if those statements don't actually support the given claim.) To address this source of confusion, show students how a statement can be true *without* supporting a claim. One way to confirm that students can distinguish between supportive and non-supportive (vs. accurate and non-accurate) statements is to make all the statements in your sample items factually accurate.

➔ Because the process of evaluating evidence prepares students to choose better evidence when crafting their own arguments, this tool supports standards and practices related to providing evidence as well as evaluating it (Common Core R.CCR.1 and 8, W.CCR.1 and 9, SL.CCR.3, and Mathematical Practice Standard 3; also Practice 7 from the Next Generation Science Standards [NGSS Lead States, 2013]).

➔ Inviting students to develop Choose Your Evidence items for each other is both fun for them and good practice. The process of developing the items and checking/discussing their partners' responses helps students get a better grasp on what does (and doesn't) count as evidence.

➔ To make the tool more hands-on, record claims, supporting statements, and irrelevant statements on strips of paper. Put the strips in a bag, and have students determine what's what. ("This strip must be the claim; this strip contains a piece of supporting evidence...") To add a level of challenge, put strips for two separate claims (and evidence to support each one) in the same bag, and ask students to determine which evidence supports which claim.

Claim Check

What is it?

A tool that trains students to investigate the validity of claims they encounter on television, on the Internet, in print, and elsewhere

What are the benefits of using this tool?

Because the ability to critically evaluate ideas is essential for college and career success (NGA Center/CCSSO, 2010), it's an ability that we must work to cultivate in our students. This tool helps by teaching students to investigate the validity of claims they encounter both in and out of the classroom. Besides supporting a number of Common Core Standards, including Reading Standard 8 and Speaking & Listening Standard 3, encouraging this kind of critical thinking prepares students "not only to engage in scholarly conversation and debate... but also to be engaged citizens in a democratic society" (Armstrong, Moyer, & Stanton, 2006, p. 1).

What are the basic steps?

1. Talk to students about the importance of evaluating the claims they encounter on TV, in texts, etc.
2. Present students with a specific claim/argument to evaluate. For example:
   - How valid is this person's claim that all birds can fly?
   - How valid is this person's claim that children your age need ten hours of sleep per night?
   - How valid is this organization's claim that vaccines cause autism?
   - How valid is this advertisement's claim that chili pepper extract can help you lose weight?
   - How valid is this article's claim that music education promotes broader academic success?
   - How valid is this writer's claim that texting and driving is more dangerous than driving drunk?
   - How valid is the congressman's claim that human activities contribute to global warming?
   - How valid is the claim that weight lifting is a better weight-loss strategy than aerobic exercise?
3. Have students search for evidence for/against the given claim and make an informed judgment about the claim's validity. Train students to consider the soundness, relevance, and sufficiency of the evidence they find (as well as the credibility of their sources) when making their judgments.

   Tip: Prepare students to be successful by modeling the process of gathering and evaluating evidence. Evaluate several claims as a class before asking students to check any on their own.
4. Ask students to explain what they decided and why. ("This claim appears to be valid because..." or "I question this claim because I found two reputable sources that contradict it.")
5. Review students' reasoning. If needed, use probing questions to help students clarify, expand, or re-evaluate their thinking. ("Should a celebrity's beliefs on this issue outweigh concrete data from the medical research community?" "Did you verify that information using multiple sources?")
6. Encourage students to check claims independently—not just when you tell them to, and not just in school, but always. ("Don't believe everything you read or hear. Check the evidence!")

How is this tool used in the classroom?

✔ To train students to think critically about claims they encounter in different contexts

Teacher Talk

➔ Need help teaching students how to assess the credibility, accuracy, and relevance of potential sources (Step 3)? Check out the Source Savvy tool (pp. 86–90).

➔ Simplify the tool as needed when using it with younger students, struggling students, or students who are just learning to evaluate claims and evidence. Here are some possible options:

- Give students claims that are easily checkable and objectively right or wrong (e.g., "All birds can fly").
- Have students evaluate claims as a class or in groups rather than on their own.
- Provide students with sources to consult ("Look for evidence in the books and articles on the back table") rather than having them search for sources on their own. Sources that don't require reading (e.g., videos, graphs, books read aloud) are ideal for very young students and struggling readers.
- Simplify the guidelines for evaluating evidence (Step 3). Instead of requiring students to consider the credibility of their sources, for example, let them use any sources they want.

➔ Talk to students about the potential value of consulting multiple sources when checking a claim.

➔ Help students appreciate the importance of evaluating things they see and hear (on TV, for example) by showing them examples of claims that *aren't* well supported by quality evidence. One option is to have them explore a fact-checking website like the Pulitzer Prize-winning PolitiFact (www.politifact.com).

➔ Use this tool to initiate a conversation about the ways that people's personal biases, points of view, or purposes might affect the claims they make or the evidence they use to support those claims. Point out that the selective use of evidence (i.e., highlighting evidence that supports a claim while ignoring contradictory evidence) is actually a very common phenomenon.

➔ Use concrete examples to help students see that searching for evidence doesn't always have to involve doing library-type research—it can involve carrying out experiments, making models, and/or performing calculations instead. ("We could check the claim that the toilet bowl is the germiest spot in a typical house by *carrying out an experiment.*")

Note: Getting students to test claims/hypotheses experimentally, and to evaluate claims in general, supports Practices 3 and 7 from the Next Generation Science Standards.

➔ Claim Check supports a number of Common Core Standards, including those that call for students to evaluate the soundness of arguments and claims (R.CCR.8, SL.CCR.3, and Mathematical Practice Standard 3); research specific questions, assess the credibility of their sources, and synthesize their findings (W.CCR.7–8); and support conclusions with source-based evidence (R.CCR.1 and W.CCR.9). Because examining and critiquing other people's arguments prepares students to craft better arguments themselves, the tool also supports Writing Standard 1.

Connection Challenge

What is it?

A tool that targets Common Core Reading Standard 3 by challenging students to identify and describe connections between items within a text—characters, events, ideas, etc.

What are the benefits of using this tool?

The release of the Common Core State Standards triggered many shifts in classroom instruction. One of these shifts involved changing the focus of text-based conversations and lessons so that there was less emphasis on making connections *to* texts (real world or personal) and more emphasis on understanding connections *within* texts. Connection Challenge supports this shift, both by introducing students to the types of in-text connections they're likely to see, and by helping students practice identifying and explaining these types of connections.

What are the basic steps?

1. Develop a question that challenges students to identify a meaningful connection between two or more items from a text (individuals, events, ideas, steps, story elements, etc.). Among other things, you might ask students to
   - Identify a connection between a story's setting and its plot.
   - Identify a connection between a specific incident and a character's state of mind.
   - Identify a relationship between two historical events.
   - Describe the relationship between a specific item and a larger category.
   - Describe the relationship between two specific steps in a process.

   Tip: If you review Common Core Reading Standard 3 across the grade levels, you'll find examples of the kinds of connections that students are expected to analyze (e.g., how setting shapes plot).

2. Pose your connection question to students. ("Do you see any connection between the Little Blue Engine's positive attitude and her ability to pull the train over the mountain?")

3. Encourage students to use connection words from the handout on p. 22 in their responses. ("Her positive attitude made it possible for her to pull the train over the mountain.")

   Note: If the handout doesn't include appropriate connection words for whatever relationship students are describing, add—or have students add—additional words.

4. Have students use specific words/details from the text to support, explain, or further clarify their responses. ("She kept telling herself, 'I think I can, I think I can.' And that helped her make it over the mountain.") Using text-based details in this way supports Common Core Reading Standard 1.

5. Work through several more "How are these items connected?" examples as a class before having students work independently. (Ideally, use examples from both literary and informational texts.) Clarify that there won't always be one right answer—that students may find different connections.

How is this tool used in the classroom?

✔ To help students recognize relationships between individuals, ideas, and other items in a text

EXAMPLE 1: Connection between an action and an outcome in a fable

QUESTION: What is the connection between the boy crying "Wolf!" and no one coming to help at the end?

RESPONSE: The boy crying "Wolf!" all the time caused no one to come help him later in the story.

EXPLANATION: The boy cried "Wolf!" so many times when a wolf wasn't there that no one believed him when he really needed help.

EXAMPLE 2: Connection between steps in a procedure

QUESTION: With regard to the order of operations, what is the relationship between the addition, subtraction, multiplication, and division steps?

RESPONSE: Multiplication and division should be done before addition and subtraction.

EXPLANATION: The order of operations tells you to handle parentheses first, then exponents, then multiplication and division. Addition and subtraction are done last.

EXAMPLE 3: Connection between an event and an individual

QUESTION: How did the ride in Frank Hawks's plane affect Amelia Earhart's life?

RESPONSE: The ride was a turning point in Earhart's life. It provoked her decision to become a pilot.

EXPLANATION: According to this biography, Earhart's earlier attendance at a stunt show had piqued her interest in flying, but it was the plane ride that sealed the deal. Earhart noted, "By the time I had got two or three hundred feet off the ground, I knew I had to fly" (http://www.ameliaearhart.com/about/bio.html).

EXAMPLE 4: Connection between two individuals

QUESTION: How would you characterize the relationship between Mary Cassatt and Edgar Degas?

RESPONSE: Cassatt and Degas had a close relationship and influenced each other's work.

EXPLANATION: According to Strasnick (2014), "their artworks…leave behind compelling clues about their friendship." One clue is Cassatt's appearance in many of Degas's paintings. Another is their parallel use of…

EXAMPLE 5: Connection between a document and a movement

QUESTION: Do you see any connection between the Treaty of Versailles and Hitler's rise to power?

RESPONSE: One could argue that the terms of the Versailles Treaty contributed to Hitler's rise to power.

EXPLANATION: According to the documentary, Hitler's desire to restore the power and glory of Germany's military appealed to Germans who were upset about the treaty's restrictions on their armed forces. Also…

EXAMPLE 6: Connection between a setting and a character's words/actions

QUESTION: Do you see any relationship between Mrs. Bennet's character and the setting of the novel?

RESPONSE: Mrs. Bennet's character—particularly her obsession with marriage—is shaped by the setting.

EXPLANATION: At the time/place where the novel is set, women like Mrs. Bennet's daughters, who weren't independently wealthy, needed to marry well in order to do well themselves. This is why Mrs. Bennet…

Teacher Talk

➔ Here are some options for younger students, struggling students, or students who are new to the tool:

- Shorten and/or simplify the list of connection words on the handout (p. 22). And don't assume that the words are self-explanatory. Explain (and use concrete examples to illustrate) their meanings.
- Make and explain connections as a class rather than having students work independently.
- Get students used to making connections by starting off with familiar items rather than items from a text. Here's an example:

  Teacher: Do you see any relationship between hard work and good grades?
  Student: Hard work contributes to good grades.

- Instead of having students generate responses from scratch, give them fill-in-the-blank statements like the ones below, and have them insert appropriate connection words. Students can fill in the blanks with words from the handout, or from a limited number of choices that you give them.
  - A bear *is an example of* an animal that hibernates.
  - The incident *colored* the narrator's outlook on life.

➔ Make students aware of common connection types by helping them group the connection words from the handout into categories and describe each category. ("Why might we put *caused, led to, provoked the decision to*, and *was the result of* into the same group? What do they have in common? All describe causal relationships.") Connection types you might come up with include cause/effect, part/whole, problem/solution, and before/after. Note that it can help to focus on one of these connection types at a time when working through examples as a class (Step 5).

➔ Since cause/effect relationships are a major component of Common Core Reading Standard 3 (they have a special place in the Next Generation Science Standards as well), you may want to give them a little extra time and attention. Several different types are highlighted in the examples on p. 20: a character's actions affecting the outcome of a story (Example 1), an event affecting an individual (Example 3), and a treaty affecting an individual's rise to power (Example 5).

➔ Need help generating your connection questions in Step 1? The table below highlights the kinds of items you might ask students to draw connections between.

Character or individual	Action or decision	Theme	Fact or bit of information
Step in a process or procedure	Line(s) of dialogue	Setting	Attitude or state of mind
Event, incident, or outcome	Hypothesis or idea	Plot element	Object or item
Opinion or point of view	Data or discovery	Personality trait	Concept or category

➔ Using the tool regularly can help students internalize both the types of relationships they're likely to encounter while reading, and the language they can use to describe those relationships.

➔ This tool focuses on the kinds of relationships discussed in Common Core Reading Standard 3—relationships between ideas, events, and individuals. To have students explore relationships between structural elements in a text (a focus of Common Core Reading Standard 5), try the Structure, Function, Relationships tool (pp. 47–49) instead.

Name: ____________________ Date: ____________

Connection Challenge

QUESTION:

RESPONSE (underline the connection words):

EXPLANATION (use specific details from the text to explain or further describe the connection or relationship):

CONNECTION WORDS (use the words on this list or generate your own):

Caused or led to	Made it possible for	Explained, clarified, or indicated	Is an example, type, or member of
Provoked the decision to	Contributed or added to	Helped to establish or confirm	Is a way to or a solution for
Influenced or shaped	Aided the development of	Suggested or supported	Is an advantage or disadvantage of
Changed or colored	Was a precursor to	Was consistent with	Is similar to or different than
Was the result or outcome of	Came before or after	Contradicted or challenged	Had a friendly or cooperative relationship
Was a turning point in	Foreshadowed	Revealed	Had an antagonistic relationship

Describe First, Compare Second

What is it?

A tool that uses a description step to help students conduct the kinds of thoughtful comparisons that Common Core Reading Standard 9 and other standards require

What are the benefits of using this tool?

Marzano, Pickering, and Pollock (2001) report that developing comparative thinking skills can have a large and positive impact on student achievement. But what does it take to actually develop these skills? This tool outlines a simple process for teaching comparison in the classroom.* The key to its success lies in its insistence on having students *describe* individual items before actually comparing them. Asking students to "describe first, compare second" is a simple instructional move, but it's one that we've seen pay off in countless numbers of classrooms with countless numbers of students.

What are the basic steps?

1. Select two items for students to compare (e.g., texts, objects, individuals, events, or concepts). Start with familiar items like plates and bowls or apples and oranges.
2. Ask students to describe each item individually using the Description Organizer (p. 27). Guide the process by providing specific attributes, components, or criteria for students to focus on (e.g., Who are the main *characters* in each story? What is the basic *plot*?).

   Note: Very young students can work through Steps 2–5 as a class, and orally rather than on paper.
3. Have students use the information on their organizers to identify ways the items are similar and different. Encourage them to focus on the components they described in Step 2 when making these comparisons (e.g., How are the *characters* in the stories similar/different? The *plots*?).
4. Have students record the similarities/differences they identify on a Comparison Organizer (p. 28).
5. Assign a writing task that requires students to synthesize what they've learned from their analysis. Here are some options (the relevant Common Core Standards are noted in parentheses):
   - Explain how the items are similar and different. (W.CCR.2)
   - Take a position on whether the items are more alike or different. Justify your position. (W.CCR.1)
   - Compare how these two authors/texts addressed this theme, topic, or event. (R.CCR.9, RI.4–5.6)
6. Encourage students to use a "describe first, compare second" approach whenever they're faced with a comparison task (e.g., on a standardized exam).
7. Prepare students to handle comparison tasks independently by training them to scan task descriptions for hints about specific attributes/components to focus on, and by discussing the kinds of attributes they might want to focus on if attributes aren't provided. See Teacher Talk for details.

---

*This process is adapted from our Compare & Contrast strategy. For more on this strategy, see *The Core Six* (Silver, Dewing, & Perini, 2012) or *Compare & Contrast: Teaching Comparative Thinking to Strengthen Student Learning* (Silver, 2010).

How is this tool used in the classroom?

- ✔ To help students handle comparison questions more successfully
- ✔ To help students conduct more focused and organized comparisons

EXAMPLE 1: Primary

A second-grade teacher addressed Common Core RL.2.9 by helping students compare two different Cinderella stories (the version popularized by Walt Disney and Rafe Martin's [1992] retelling of an Algonquin version). The Description and Comparison Organizers that they generated as a class are shown below. The comparison paragraph that one student used these organizers to write is shown on the next page.

Notice how the aspects of the stories that students described in the Description Organizer became the focus for both the Comparison Organizer *and* the final written piece. (In other words, students described, then compared, then wrote about the same five things: main characters, personalities, wants, ending, and lesson.) Teaching students to do this same thing—to use their organizers to guide the pieces that they write—will help them produce higher-quality comparison essays.

DESCRIPTION ORGANIZER

Story 1: Cinderella	Describe these things:	Story 2: The Rough-Face Girl
Cinderella two stepsisters prince fairy godmother	Main characters	Rough-Face Girl two sisters Invisible Being
Cinderella is good and sweet. Her stepsisters are mean.	What the three sisters are like	The Rough-Face girl has a kind heart. Her sisters are mean.
They all want to marry the prince.	What the three sisters want	They all want to marry the Invisible Being.
The prince marries Cinderella instead of the mean sisters. They live happily ever after.	How the story ends	The Invisible Being marries the Rough-Face Girl instead of the mean sisters. They live happily ever after.
Good things happen to good people.	Lesson of the story	Good things happen to good people.

COMPARISON ORGANIZER ("TOP HAT" FORMAT)

Ways the stories are different	Cinderella:	The Rough-Face Girl:
	Cinderella has a fairy godmother to help her.	The Rough-Face Girl doesn't have a fairy godmother.
	Cinderella wants to marry a prince.	The Rough-Face Girl wants to marry the Invisible Being.

Ways the stories are alike:
In both stories, the main character is nice and her sisters are mean.
In both stories, the main character and her sisters want to marry the same person.
Both stories end the same way. The nice sister gets married and lives happily ever after. The mean sisters don't.
Both stories teach the same lesson that good things happen to good people.

COMPARISON PARAGRAPH

I am comparing two Cinderella storys. One is called Cinderella. The other is the rought face girl. One way both storys are alike is that the main character has two mean sisters. A second way they are alike is that in both storys all the sisters what to mary the same person but only the nice sisters gets to mary him at the end. Another way they are alike is that both storys teach you the same losson. Something that is differnt is Cinderella has a fairy god mother to help her and the rought face girl dosent but for the other resons I told you these two storys are a lot alike.

EXAMPLE 2: Elementary

A third-grade teacher used this tool to help her students analyze the development of a character over the course of a text (Common Core R.CCR.3). She did this by having them compare Wilbur from Chapter 7 of *Charlotte's Web* (White, 1952) with Wilbur from Chapter 15. The Comparison Organizer that one of her students generated can be seen at www.ThoughtfulClassroom.com/Tools.

EXAMPLE 3: Secondary

A middle school teacher designed the following comparative writing task around a segment of *Alive: The Story of the Andes Survivors* (Read, 1974/2002): "Compare Canessa and Parrado as expeditionaries. Consider the following attributes when making your comparison: physical strength, attitude, and knowledge." The Description Organizer that one student generated in preparation for this task is shown below. Notice how he recorded the page numbers where he found key details so he'd have an easier time referring to those details in his essay.

DESCRIPTION ORGANIZER

Character #1:	Describe these attributes:	Character #2:
Parrado		Canessa
• always taking the lead and going 1st (280-81) • motivated/strong	← physical st. →	• was always falling down and becoming weak. (281) • tired/diarrhea (290)
• thinking about dad • motivated to keep going • happy when saw animals, green, can (285)	← attitude →	• thinking about God • wanted to keep on taking breaks • sad/mad and shouted "You'll kill yourself!" (284)
• had dumb ideas about killing cow, but was still motivated (295)	← knowledge →	• med. student • knew about vitamins, protiens, cow dung (289)

Teacher Talk

➔ The ability to compare is key to Common Core success. We see this most obviously with Reading Standard 9, but specific grade-level expectations within Reading Standards 3, 5, 6, and 7 require comparison as well. (RI.4.6, for example, requires students to compare different accounts of an event or topic.) Comparative writing is also required by the Common Core; it's part of Writing Standard 2.

➔ Prepare students to produce quality work by showing them examples of well-written comparison pieces, discussing the pieces' basic components and structures, and familiarizing students with linking/organizing words they can use to highlight similarities and differences (see p. 77 for a list).

➔ When students are conducting text-based comparisons, encourage them to include specific details and snippets from the texts on their organizers. Noting the page numbers where these items appear, as shown in Example 3, helps students incorporate these details into their final pieces. Building these details into their responses addresses Common Core Writing Standard 9 and Reading Standard 1.

➔ Clarify that the word "comparing" typically implies comparing *and* contrasting. ("If a question or prompt asks you to *compare* two things, you should discuss the similarities *and* the differences.")

➔ Use concrete examples like these to show students how test questions/task descriptions sometimes point to specific elements that they should focus on when conducting their comparisons:

Task 1: Compare the kinds of adaptations that enable the animals you read about to survive in their various habitats. You may wish to address adaptations involved in finding food, regulating body temperature, or avoiding predators. (Here, the task suggests specific kinds of adaptations that students might want to compare.)

Task 2: Compare George Washington's Farewell Address to the Monroe Doctrine. Analyze how both texts address similar themes and concepts regarding "entangling alliances."* (Here, the task asks students to focus on what the individual documents have to say about entangling alliances.)

➔ Talk to students about elements they might want to compare if none are suggested by the test question or task. For example:

- If you're asked to compare two *characters*, you might compare their personalities, adventures, experiences, or interactions with other characters.
- If you're asked to compare two *fictional texts*, you might compare their plots, settings, characters, themes, lessons/morals, illustrations, and/or writing styles.
- If you're asked to compare two *informational texts*, you might compare their factual content, structures, purposes, points of view, and/or quality of evidence.

➔ Use specific examples to teach students that comparative writing tasks won't always contain the words *compare* and *contrast*. Here is how a ninth-grade teacher did this using a task designed around Common Core RL.9–10.7:

"This task is asking you to analyze representations of the fall of man in two different artistic mediums, including what is emphasized or absent in each one. The word *comparison* doesn't appear anywhere in the task description, but it's a comparison task nonetheless. How can we tell?"

*This task is adapted from Appendix B of the Common Core ELA/Literacy Standards, p. 129.

Name: Date:

Description Organizer

Item or text #1:	Describe these attributes, aspects, or components:	Item or text #2:

Name: Date:

"Top Hat" Comparison Organizer

Differences:

Item or text #1:

Item or text #2:

Similarities:

Four for Fluency

What is it?

A tool for targeting the fluency component of the Common Core Reading Standards

What are the benefits of using this tool?

Fluency—or the ability to read effortlessly, with speed, accuracy, and proper expression—is a key skill that can affect students' understanding and enjoyment of what they read. Unfortunately, it's also a skill that many students struggle with. The good news is that fluency can be improved, and we know how to go about doing it (National Reading Panel, 2000). This tool presents four simple techniques for promoting fluency in the classroom. These techniques work by helping students hear what fluent reading sounds like, and by giving them multiple opportunities to practice and improve their oral reading skills.

What are the basic steps?

1. Explain what fluency is and why it's important to develop. For example, "It's a lot easier to 'get' a text if you don't have to stop every few seconds to figure out what a word is and how to say it!"
2. Assess fluency by having students read grade-level-appropriate texts aloud. Pay attention to rate, accuracy, and expression. (Do students adjust their tone to match the words they're reading? Pause at appropriate places? Read words in meaningful groups rather than one by one?)
3. Familiarize yourself with the oral reading techniques described on p. 31, and begin using them (focus on one, or try a variety) with individual students or groups of students. Use the data you gathered in Step 2 to determine which students need the most practice, and be sure they get it.

   Tip: Adjust text complexity and instructional time as needed to ensure that students at all levels are both challenged and supported.
4. Discuss and model strategies for addressing common fluency problems, and encourage students to use these strategies independently. Here are some possibilities (adapted from Reutzel, 2006):
   - Slow down when the text is difficult or unfamiliar.
   - Take a big breath. Try to read to the comma or end punctuation before taking another breath.
   - Try to sound like someone talking when you read.
   - Make the sound of each letter and blend the sounds quickly to say the word.
   - Listen to what you've read. Does it make sense? If not, try reading it again before asking for help.
5. Reassess students' skills on a regular basis. Adjust instructional groups, amount of practice time, and text complexity accordingly.

How is this tool used in the classroom?

✔ To model fluent reading and help students become more fluent readers

Teacher Talk

- ➔ Haven't devoted that much time to oral reading instruction before? Do it now! Guided oral reading techniques have been found to have a "consistent and positive impact on word recognition, fluency, and comprehension" as well as overall reading achievement (National Reading Panel, 2000, p. 3–3). They're also great for addressing the fluency component of the Common Core Reading Standards (specifically, standard RF.1–5.4b).

- ➔ The concept of reading with proper expression is one that needs to be taught explicitly and modeled regularly. When reading texts aloud, stop periodically to explain why you're reading in a particular way.

  Sample language: Did you notice that I paused when I came to the period at the end of the sentence? A period signals a break, so we pause just a bit.

  Sample language: Did you hear how I put some extra emphasis on the word *can*? When a word appears in italics, like that one did, we give it a little extra oomph.

- ➔ When reading aloud, remember to read at a pace that's appropriate for your students (typically slower than your natural pace). If you read too quickly, the benefits may be lost.

- ➔ Prepare students for success by identifying, pronouncing, and defining challenging words *before* they begin reading.

- ➔ Although the Common Core State Standards' emphasis on fluency ends in the fifth grade, many students (particularly low achievers, English language learners, and those with learning disabilities) struggle with fluency issues well beyond elementary school. For this reason, we recommend that teachers at all grade levels assess and address potential fluency issues.

- ➔ To assess fluency quantitatively, you can score "words correct per minute" (WCPM). (Instructions and WCPM norms by grade level are readily available online. Keep in mind, though, that this method of assessing fluency doesn't take expression into account.) Another option is to use a fluency rubric; see Rasinski's (2004) "Creating Fluent Readers" for a good example.

- ➔ To boost engagement, let *students* choose which oral reading technique(s) to use in Step 3. Another way to boost engagement? Select (or let students help you select) texts that they're interested in.

- ➔ Looking to add a technology component? Have students listen to recorded selections at home while following along on paper (research by Blum et al., 1995, and Martinez & Barnhill, 2011, suggests this may be beneficial for both native English speakers and English language learners)—or have students record themselves reading and play the recordings back to hear how they're doing. Address Common Core Speaking & Listening Standard SL.3.5 by challenging students to create engaging recordings that demonstrate fluid reading at an appropriate pace.

Four Techniques for Fostering Fluency

Listen-Follow-Read (LFR)

LFR involves modeling and having students imitate fluent reading. Here are the basic steps:

1. Distribute copies of a short text or excerpt (< 250 words) to a student or group of students.
2. Ask students to listen carefully as you read the text aloud. Read with expression, and instruct them to pay attention to what you're doing with your voice. Call their attention to the way you pause at commas and periods, lift your voice slightly when you encounter a question mark, emphasize some words more than others, etc.
3. Read the text again. Instruct students to follow along on the printed text, pointing to each word and punctuation mark as you read. Check that you're reading slowly enough for students to do this, and that all students are participating.
4. When you finish, ask students to read the text back to you, one student at a time. Encourage students to match the rate and expression of your initial readings.
5. Give students feedback about their performance and the opportunity to try again, particularly if they struggled the first time.

Paired Repeated Reading

Paired Repeated Reading (Koskinen & Blum, 1986) is a cooperative technique that can be used relatively quickly and with minimal supervision. Here are the basic steps:

1. Group students into pairs. Give each student a Reading Sheet and a Listening Sheet; both can be found on p. 32.
2. Have each student select a different passage to read aloud. Passages should be approximately fifty words in length, and at a level where mastery is possible. (Giving students some options can facilitate the selection process.)
3. Give students time to read their passages silently, then decide which member of the pair will read first (the other student will be the "listener"). Readers should read their passages aloud three times in row and rate each performance on the Reading Sheet. (Readers are welcome to ask their partners for assistance while reading.) Listeners should tell the readers how their reading improved each time and mark the Listening Sheet accordingly.
4. After the third reading, have readers and listeners exchange roles and repeat the process.

Note: Be sure to discuss and model the criteria on the Reading and Listening Sheets before students begin working. ("What does it mean to read something with expression? Let's see…") You may want to model the entire technique as well—read the same passage three times through, do a better job each time, and ask students to score your performance accordingly.

Choral Reading

Choral Reading involves reading aloud as a group. Here are the basic steps:

1. Distribute a short text to the entire class. Model fluent reading by reading the text aloud.
2. Read the text a second time, and have everyone read along with you. Encourage students to mimic your pace, inflection, and tone.
3. Read the text a few more times as a group (same day or later in the week). Then, instruct students to read it softly to themselves. Encourage them to aim for accuracy while mimicking the pace and expression of the group readings.

Echo Reading

Echo Reading is similar to Choral Reading, but it can be used with slightly longer texts. Use it exactly like Choral Reading, but move through the text two to four sentences at a time instead of reading the entire text in one pass.

Reading Sheet

This Reading Sheet belongs to ______________________________ .

THINK: Did I read the words *correctly*, *smoothly*, and *with expression*? How did I do overall?

How did I do the FIRST time I read?	Great!	Pretty well	OK	Needed work
How did I do the SECOND time I read?	Great!	Pretty well	OK	Needed work
How did I do the THIRD time I read?	Great!	Pretty well	OK	Needed work

How did I improve? What could I do to improve further?

cut here

Listening Sheet

This Listening Sheet belongs to ______________________________ .

Today, I listened to this person read: ______________________________ .

How did my partner improve on the SECOND reading?

- ☐ Knew more words
- ☐ Read more smoothly
- ☐ Read more quickly
- ☐ Read with better expression

How did my partner improve on the THIRD reading?

- ☐ Knew more words
- ☐ Read more smoothly
- ☐ Read more quickly
- ☐ Read with better expression

Note: The reproducibles on this page are adapted from the work of Koskinen and Blum (1986).

Main Idea

What is it?

A guided approach to helping students identify main ideas

What are the benefits of using this tool?

Teaching students to identify main ideas and supporting details has been a classroom priority for years, and that focus is unlikely to change given the inclusion of main-idea identification skills in the Common Core Reading Standards (Standard 2). Despite our best efforts, however, many students still struggle to find main ideas. This tool helps by outlining a concrete process for identifying main ideas, by modeling that process in detail, and by prescribing ongoing instruction and practice using increasingly challenging examples.

What are the basic steps?

1. Discuss the difference between the *topic* of a reading (the subject of that reading) and the *main idea* (the central point the reading is making about that topic).

2. Teach students that they can help themselves find main ideas by following three simple steps:

- Identify the topic by asking yourself, "Who or what is this reading about?"
- Identify the main idea by asking yourself, "What is the main thing the reading is telling me about this topic?"
- Check your work by asking, "Can I find facts or examples that support my main idea?" If you can't find several supporting details, you might need to rethink your main idea!

3. Model these three steps using a sample text, and use the Main Idea Organizer on p. 36 to record your ideas. Encourage students to chime in and help you as you work.

Tip: The texts you use for your initial modeling sessions should have clearly stated main ideas and easy-to-find supporting details. You can use single paragraphs, short passages, or whole texts.

4. Give students opportunities to practice the three-step process with similarly clear and simple examples (as a class, in groups, then on their own). Provide feedback and assistance as needed.

5. Model the three-step process using progressively longer and more complex readings (readings in which the main idea isn't in the topic sentence, isn't explicitly stated, etc.). Explain that some passages have more than one main idea, and show students examples of those as well.

Tip: Prepare students for success by teaching them tips for identifying main ideas in complex passages. See Teacher Talk for suggestions.

6. Give students opportunities to practice and get feedback with similarly complex passages—as a class, in groups, and then on their own. Be sure the passages you select actually have main ideas (a simple descriptive passage, for example, might not).

How is this tool used in the classroom?

✔ To help students identify main ideas and supporting details

EXAMPLE 1: Primary science*

Although main-idea identification skills aren't required by the Common Core Reading Standards (Informational Text) until third grade, you can build these skills earlier if you guide students through the process. Here's how a second-grade teacher did this with a passage she read aloud from *Reptiles Do the Strangest Things* (Hornblow & Hornblow, 1970):

Teacher: Before we can identify the main idea, we need to figure out the topic. To do this, we ask ourselves who or what the reading is about. Here, everything seems to be about…

Students: Hog-nose snakes!

Teacher: Correct! Let's write *hog-nose snakes* in the "topic box" of our organizer.

Next, we should ask ourselves, "What's the main thing this passage is telling us about hog-nose snakes?" I think it's saying that hog-nose snakes do some really strange things to protect themselves from being eaten by enemies. Do you agree? Good! Let's write that idea in the main-idea box.

Finally, we should check our work by seeing if we can find any facts or examples to support our main idea. Do you see any examples of strange things these snakes do to protect themselves?

Students: Yes! They puff up their bodies… lash their tails…hiss… play dead… lie upside down…

This teacher recorded her students' ideas on the organizer as they shouted them out. She then concluded her lesson by reviewing the three questions that she and her students had used to help them find the main idea: (1) Who or what is the reading about? (2) What is the main thing the reading is telling us about this topic? (3) Is there information in the reading to support our main idea?

EXAMPLE 2: Secondary history

A world history student generated this organizer after reading an assigned passage in her textbook:

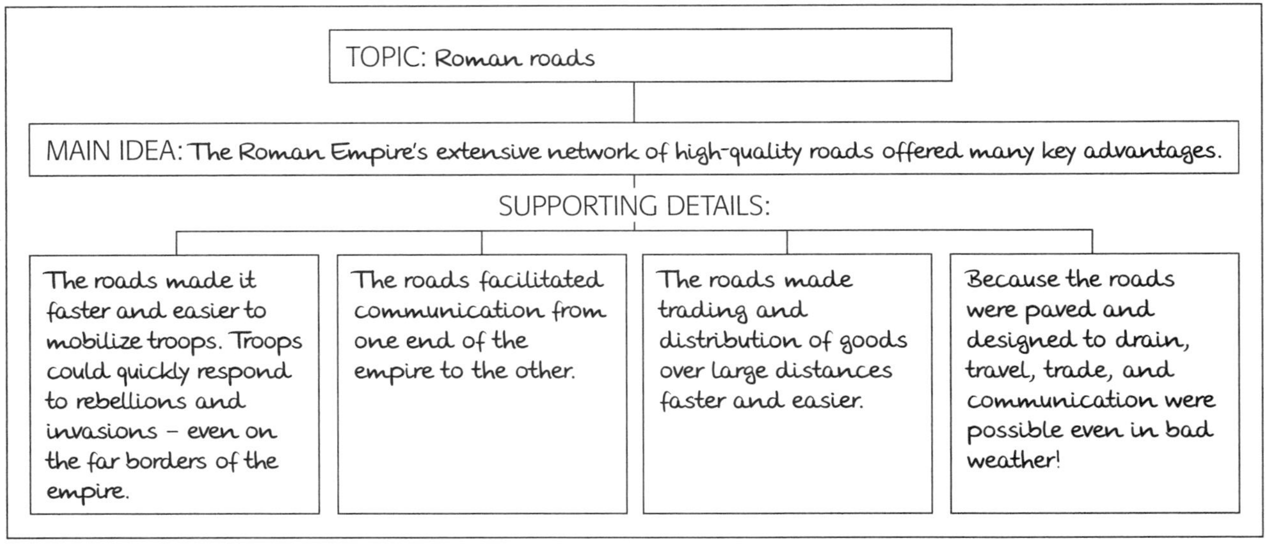

*This lesson is adapted from *Discovering Nonfiction: 25 Powerful Teaching Strategies, Grades 2–6* (Silver, Strong, & Perini, 2000, p.11).

Teacher Talk

➔ Teach students specific tips and strategies for finding main ideas in complex passages. Share strategies that you use (explain them during the modeling process), or try some of these:

- Teach students to look for clues in introductory sentences and paragraphs, summary sentences and paragraphs, section headings, and specially formatted bits of text (e.g., italicized, bold, large font).
- Explain that the structure of a text (e.g., comparison, cause/effect, argument) can sometimes offer clues to the main idea as well. With a cause/effect paragraph, for example, the main idea will likely be about the causes and/or effects of the general topic. ("The Civil War had many causes.")
- Remind students to look beyond the opening sentence when searching for main ideas. Dispel the myth that main ideas are always found at the beginning of a paragraph by showing students specific examples in which the main idea is stated elsewhere. And clarify that in some texts, the main idea won't be explicitly stated *anywhere* (i.e., students will have to infer it).
- Since some students have an easier time formulating main ideas if they think of them as summary statements, encourage students to ask themselves this: "If I had to summarize the main point of this passage in a single sentence, what would I say?"
- If students are struggling, it may help to have them complete the details portion of the organizer first and work backwards to get the main idea. To scaffold this process, you can underline key terms and details for them, and help them use those terms/details to identify the main idea. ("What do the underlined bits have in common? What's the big idea that holds them together?")

➔ Other scaffolding options:

- Focus on one skill at a time. For example, *give* students the main idea (rather than asking them to find it) so they can just practice identifying supporting details.
- Let students select the main idea (or topic or details) from a list of choices rather than come up with these items from scratch. (Besides being easier, the multiple-choice format is good practice for standardized tests.) If you use this option, be sure to have students explain their choices so you can check and correct their thinking as needed. ("I circled choice *D* because...")

➔ Use concrete examples to explain—and test students' ability to recognize—the difference between a main idea and a detail. ("How can we tell that 'some animals hibernate' is a detail rather than a main idea? Is the main point of the book that some animals hibernate?")

➔ Prepare students to handle main-idea questions regardless of how they're worded by clarifying that *main idea* and *central idea* are typically synonymous terms.

➔ Move beyond basic printed texts. The ability to identify main ideas and details in different types of sources (e.g., video clips, data tables, slide shows, texts that have been read aloud) is an important one to develop, and a component of Common Core Speaking & Listening Standard 2.

Name: Date:

Main Idea Organizer

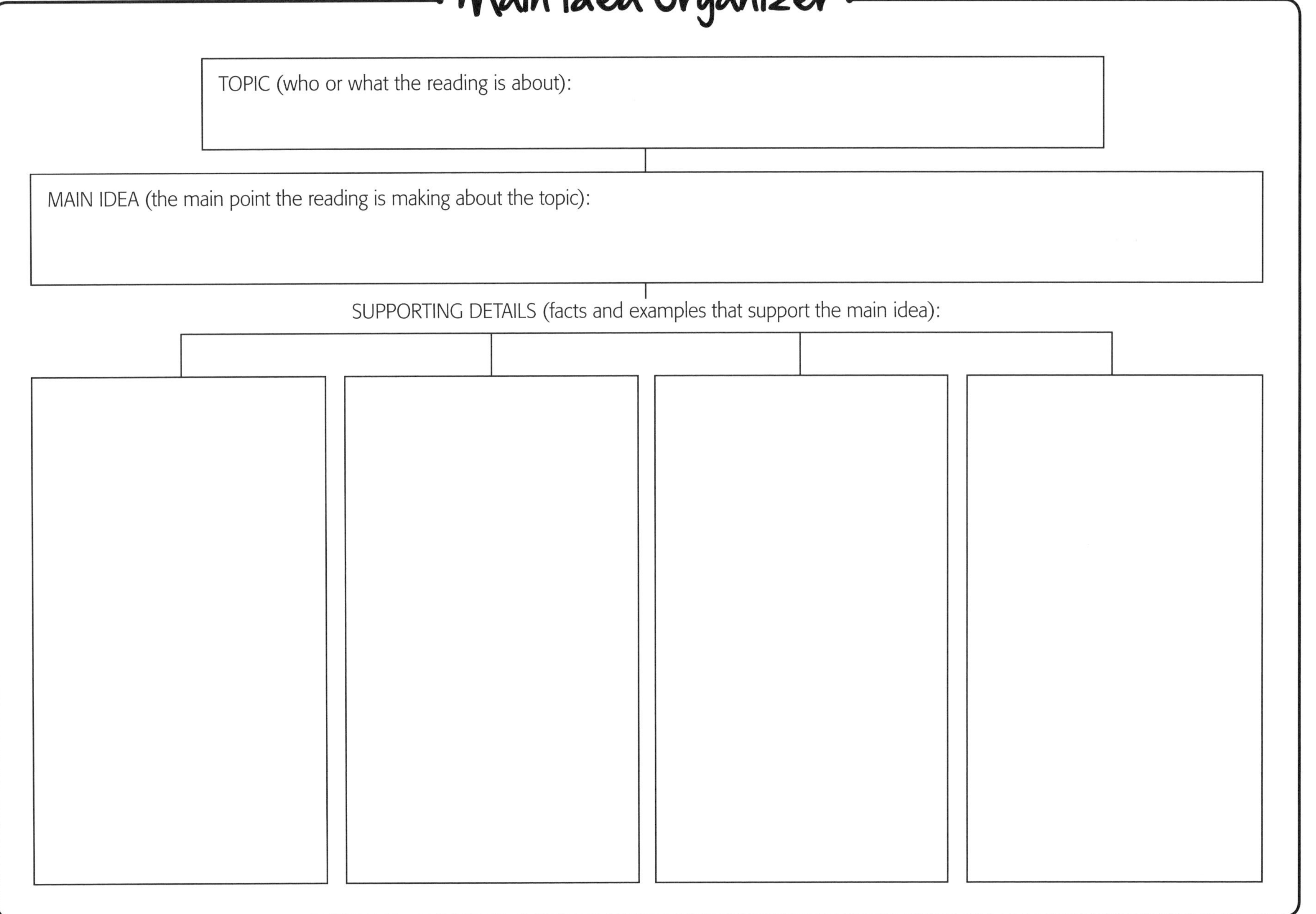

Reading for Meaning

What is it?

A tool that promotes close and active reading of assigned texts by having students examine a series of statements, decide whether they agree or disagree with each one, and cite specific evidence to support their positions*

What are the benefits of using this tool?

Both common sense and the Common Core State Standards underscore the importance of preparing students to understand and interpret critical texts. This tool helps us achieve this goal by building the exact types of skills that the Common Core has identified as critical for students' success—skills like reading closely, making inferences, and supporting those inferences with evidence (see Reading Standard 1). Plus, by teaching students to support their positions with evidence and examples (a goal of Writing Standard 1), the tool prepares them to be better writers as well as better readers.

What are the basic steps?

1. Identify a short text or portion of a text that you want students to "read for meaning." Any kind of text is fine—poem, Internet article, primary document, fable, scene from a play, etc.
2. Generate a list of statements about the text. (Students will ultimately search the text for evidence that supports and/or refutes each statement.)
   - Statements can be true, false, or open to interpretation/designed to provoke debate.
   - Statements can be customized to fit whatever skills, standards, or objectives you're trying to address (e.g., identifying main ideas or interpreting data tables). See Teacher Talk for details.
3. Tell students to preview the statements *before* they begin reading. Ask them to collect evidence that supports or refutes each statement either *as* or *after* they read. Clarify that evidence should include specific words/phrases/details from the text.
4. Have students decide whether they agree or disagree with each statement based on the evidence they've collected. (This can be done individually or in pairs/small groups.) If they can't decide, challenge them to rewrite problematic statements in a way that allows for a clear decision.
5. Invite students to share and justify their positions, either as a class or in writing. Help them clarify their thinking, and call their attention to evidence they might have missed or misinterpreted.
6. Use students' responses to evaluate both their understanding of what they've read and their ability to support a statement with textual evidence.

*For more on the Reading for Meaning technique, which is adapted from Harold Herber's Reading and Reasoning Guides (Herber, 1970), see *Reading for Meaning: How to Build Students' Comprehension, Reasoning, and Problem-Solving Skills* (Silver, Morris, & Klein, 2010) or *The Thoughtful Education Guide to Reading for Meaning* (Silver, Reilly, & Perini, 2009).

How is this tool used in the classroom?

✔ To develop and test students' ability to understand and interpret what they've read

✔ To develop and test students' ability to support a position with evidence

EXAMPLE 1: Primary ELA

After listening to the Native American folktale "Turtle Races with Beaver," second-grade students indicated whether they agreed or disagreed with five statements their teacher had generated. They then drew the evidence that led them to agree or disagree with each statement. The "picture evidence" that one student provided for the statement "Turtle won the race fairly" is shown here:

SOURCE: From *The Thoughtful Education Guide to Reading for Meaning* (p. 59), by H. F. Silver, E. C. Reilly, and M. J. Perini, 2009, Thousand Oaks, CA: Corwin Press. © 2009 by Thoughtful Education Press. Reprinted with permission.

EXAMPLE 2: Secondary ELA

An English teacher used this tool to test his students' understanding of a scene from Shakespeare's *Romeo and Juliet* (Act III, Scene II). A portion of one student's work is shown here:

Evidence for	Statements	Evidence against
The way she talks about Romeo is over the top. Sounds like teenage infatuation: "Take him and cut him out in little stars, / And he will make the face of heaven so fine, / That all the world will be in love with night, / And pay no worship to the garish sun."	Juliet's soliloquy (lines 1–31) reveals how young and naïve she is.	Her ability to express her love is not childish at all. The language is amazing!
When she finds out Romeo killed Tybalt, she seems conflicted: "Oh that deceit should dwell / In such a gorgeous place." Then she takes Romeo's side and reaffirms her love for him (lines 90–127).	Juliet's attitude toward Romeo changes over the course of the scene.	

SOURCE: Adapted from *Reading for Meaning: How to Build Students' Comprehension, Reasoning, and Problem-Solving Skills* (p. 14), by H. F. Silver, S. C. Morris, and V. Klein, 2010, Alexandria, VA: ASCD. © 2010 by Silver Strong & Associates. Adapted with permission.

EXAMPLE 3: Secondary mathematics

Math students were told to use their knowledge of probability, as well as information from a reading on the multistate lottery known as Powerball, to support or refute each statement.

Statements	Explanation/Evidence
All you need to calculate your odds of winning is basic multiplication. ☐ Agree ☐ Disagree	
You have a greater probability of winning the grand prize if you live in a big city than in a small town. ☐ Agree ☐ Disagree	

SOURCE: Adapted from *Styles and Strategies for Teaching Middle School Mathematics* (p. 52), by E. J. Thomas and J. R. Brunsting, 2010, Thousand Oaks, CA: Corwin Press. © 2010 by Thoughtful Education Press. Adapted with permission.

EXAMPLE 4: Secondary history

A US history teacher uses this tool to develop and test students' ability to analyze seminal documents of historical and literary significance (Common Core RI.9–10.9, also RI.11–12.6). One student's partially completed organizer for Lincoln's Gettysburg Address is shown below.

Statements	Agree or disagree? Support your position with evidence.
The primary goal of the speech was to honor the soldiers who had fought and died.	I disagree since the speech seems to be more a call to action than a memorial. Lincoln charges the living with dedicating themselves to the cause for which the fallen soldiers "gave the last full measure of devotion" and the task of ensuring that "government of the people, by the people, and for the people shall not perish from the earth."
Lincoln believed that our nation was at a crossroads.	
The style of the speech (in addition to its content) contributes to its power, persuasiveness, and beauty.	
Lincoln believed that the outcome of the war had implications for the entire world, not just the United States.	
Lincoln took his listeners on a journey through time.	

SOURCE: Adapted from *Tools for Thoughtful Assessment* (p. 101), by A. L. Boutz, H. F. Silver, J. W. Jackson, and M. J. Perini, 2012, Ho-Ho-Kus, NJ: Thoughtful Education Press. © 2012 by Silver Strong & Associates. Adapted with permission.

EXAMPLE 5: Elementary social studies

A fifth-grade teacher uses Reading for Meaning statements like the ones below to target Common Core Reading Standard 7, which requires students to evaluate content that's presented visually and/or quantitatively (e.g., via graphs, charts, maps, or data tables).

Statements	Evidence/Calculations
1. Seattle receives more precipitation in a year than Boston. ☐ Agree ☐ Disagree	
2. Over the course of a year, Denver sees more snow than rain. ☐ Agree ☐ Disagree	
3. On average, January is the coldest month. ☐ Agree ☐ Disagree	
4. If you were spending Independence Day in Boston, the temperature would not be above 81°F. ☐ Agree ☐ Disagree	

		Month											
City	**Avg.**	**JAN**	**FEB**	**MAR**	**APR**	**MAY**	**JUN**	**JUL**	**AUG**	**SEP**	**OCT**	**NOV**	**DEC**
Boston	*Precip.*	3.6	3.6	3.7	3.6	3.3	3.1	2.8	3.3	3.1	3.3	4.3	4.0
	Low	21	24	31	40	48	58	65	64	56	46	38	26
	High	35	37	45	55	66	76	81	78	72	62	52	40
Denver	*Precip.*	0.5	0.6	1.3	1.7	2.4	1.8	1.9	1.5	1.3	1.0	0.9	0.6
	Low	16	20	25	34	44	52	58	56	47	36	25	17
	High	44	46	52	61	70	81	88	85	76	66	52	44
Seattle	*Precip.*	5.4	4.0	3.5	2.3	1.7	1.5	0.8	1.1	1.9	3.3	5.8	5.9
	Low	35	37	38	41	46	51	55	55	51	45	40	35
	High	45	48	52	57	64	68	75	75	68	58	50	45

Average temperatures recorded in degrees Fahrenheit (ºF)
Average precipitation amounts recorded in inches (in.)

SOURCE: From *Reading for Meaning: How to Build Students' Comprehension, Reading, and Problem-Solving Skills* (p. 15), by H. F. Silver, S. C. Morris, and V. Klein, 2010, Alexandria, VA: ASCD. © 2010 by Silver Strong & Associates. Reprinted with permission.

Teacher Talk

→ Be creative! Instead of having students read and analyze a single text, have them analyze pieces of art, demonstrations, pairs of texts, or data files. See how one teacher did this in Example 5.

→ Don't assume that students know how to find evidence in a text. Explain, model, and practice this critical skill until students are comfortable with it.

→ If you're having trouble generating statements (Step 2), generate checking-for-understanding questions instead—and then turn those questions into statements. (*Question:* Who is the wisest character in this folktale? ⟶ *Statement:* The wisest character in this folktale is the grandfather.)

→ Adapt the tool as needed for developing readers. Primary-grade teachers may want to read their texts aloud (or use picture books), have students search for evidence and complete the organizer as a class, or let students draw their evidence rather than writing it (see Example 1). Scaffold the evidence-gathering process for students until they're capable of doing it on their own.

→ Statements can be designed to fit whatever skills you're addressing (e.g., identifying main ideas or summarizing facts). They can also be designed around any of the Common Core Anchor Standards for Reading—and for literary as well as informational texts (see below for examples).

Anchor-Standard Concepts	Sample Statements
Determine what a text says explicitly. (R.CCR.1)	• Everyone is unkind to the ugly duckling. • All isotopes are radioactive.
Make logical inferences from a text. (R.CCR.1)	• We can tell that Pooh and Piglet have been friends for a long time. • Without taking Franklin's data, Watson and Crick wouldn't have succeeded.
Identify main ideas and themes. (R.CCR.2)	• The moral of the story is that you should be kind to everyone. • Structure and function are intricately linked.
Analyze how and why individuals, events, and ideas develop, connect, and interact. (R.CCR.3)	• After Maxim's revelation, the new Mrs. de Winter is a changed woman. • The seeds of social change for women in America were planted during WWII.
Assess how point of view or purpose shapes the content and style of a text; distinguish between what is said and what is meant or true. (R.CCR.6)	• When the narrator notes that Della and Jim "most unwisely sacrificed for each other the greatest treasures of their house," he is expressing disapproval. • The writer's personal feelings influenced his description of this event.
Integrate and evaluate content that is presented visually and quantitatively as well as in words. (R.CCR.7)	• Ferdinand is not his usual self in this picture. • According to Table 2 from this article, sun worshippers would be happier living in Phoenix than Seattle.
Evaluate the argument and specific claims in a text. (R.CCR.8)	• The author provides sufficient evidence to support his claim. • The argument in Source 1 is stronger than the argument in Source 2.
Analyze how two or more texts address similar themes or topics in order to build knowledge or compare the authors' approaches. (R.CCR.9)	• Myths from different cultures have similar elements and themes. • The Cherokee people's account of their relocation differs from the account in your textbook.

SOURCE: Adapted from *Tools for Thoughtful Assessment* (p. 102), by A. L. Boutz, H. F. Silver, J. W. Jackson, and M. J. Perini, 2012, Ho-Ho-Kus, NJ: Thoughtful Education Press. © 2012 by Silver Strong & Associates. Adapted with permission.

Scavenger Hunt

What is it?

A fun and engaging technique for practicing text-based search tasks with ties to the Common Core Reading Standards (find a central idea, find a detail to support that idea, etc.)

What are the benefits of using this tool?

Looking at the Common Core Reading Standards can change our notion of a text from "something to be read" to "something to be searched through." Among other things, the standards require students to look for ideas, evidence, details, and claims. This tool lets students practice these kinds of text searches, and it uses a scavenger hunt format to make these searches both engaging and fun. ("Your challenge is to find the following items: a detail to support this conclusion, a sentence that reveals the author's point of view, and a portion of the text that's structured chronologically.") Because students' ability to complete these kinds of "find-it tasks" gives us valuable insight into their command of the corresponding skills, we can adjust our instruction accordingly.

What are the basic steps?

1. Identify one or more reading standards that you've been working on with your students.
2. Design some "Find a ___" tasks that have ties to the selected standard(s). Tasks should be designed around one or more grade-appropriate texts/passages, and should require searching those texts or passages for something specific. See p. 42 for examples.
3. Record your tasks on the Scavenger Hunt form (p. 44), and give students copies. Tell students whether to hunt for the items on their own or in teams, show them how to mark what they find (e.g., write on the text or use sticky notes), and clarify that accuracy is more important than speed.
4. Give students copies of the text(s) they'll need to complete the assigned tasks, and instruct them to start hunting! If appropriate, number individual lines/paragraphs so students can more easily refer to what they've found. ("The words I chose are in lines 2 and 3 of paragraph 4.")
5. Review and discuss students' responses as a class. ("Who wants to share what they found for this task?" "Can you explain why you selected this paragraph?" "Might this sentence be a better choice than that one? Why?" "Could both Sarah's and John's selections be correct? Why or why not?")
6. Encourage students to debate and defend conflicting responses (moderate as needed). Help them understand why one response is better than another or why multiple responses are equally valid.

   Note: Teaching students to express and evaluate ideas in a respectful manner supports Common Core Speaking & Listening Standards 1 and 3.
7. Collect and review students' work to gain additional information about students' mastery of specific skills (e.g., which students are still having trouble finding details to support a main idea). Work with students individually or as a class to develop any skills that students haven't yet mastered.

How is this tool used in the classroom?

✔ To get students in the habit of searching texts for specific features, information, and evidence

✔ To assess and improve students' ability to handle text-based questions

With a little creativity, you can design find-it tasks with ties to any of the Common Core Anchor Standards for Reading, and for both literary and informational texts. Here are some ideas:

To focus on individual anchor standards, challenge students to...	Sample tasks
Search for factual information and explanations that are explicitly stated within the text. (R.CCR.1)	• How did Pascal keep his red balloon dry? FIND a picture that tells us. • Why is the USS *Constitution* called "Old Ironsides"? FIND the explanation. • FIND two human behaviors/activities that contribute to global warming.
Find textual evidence to support inferences and conclusions. (R.CCR.1)	• FIND two words or pictures that might lead us to infer that the bear is angry. • FIND two sentences from the passage that support the following conclusion... • FIND one detail from each source that supports the answer to Part A.
Identify central ideas and themes, and summarize supporting details and ideas. (R.CCR.2)	• FIND the paragraph that best reflects the main idea of the passage as a whole. • Read the main idea below. FIND two details from the text that support this idea.
Find details that reveal important information about (or highlight relationships between) characters, settings, events, and individuals. (R.CCR.3)	• How can we tell the narrator is a generous individual? FIND some evidence. • FIND two details from the story that help create the setting. • FIND lines in the poem that reveal the effect the incident had on the narrator. • How did Franklin's work influence Watson and Crick? FIND some evidence.
Find clues to the meaning of words and phrases as they're used in a text or words that affect tone. (R.CCR.4)	• FIND a phrase that helps us grasp the meaning of *savage* as it's used here. • FIND words that contribute to the informal tone of this letter.
Identify and compare text structures, find connections between individual sentences or sections, and recognize how individual elements/sections contribute to the development of ideas and/or fit into the overall text structure. (R.CCR.5)	• FIND the portion of this passage that is structured chronologically. • In this passage, the author discusses two seemingly unrelated concepts. How does he connect them? FIND a sentence that makes this connection. • Examine the colonists' argument for independence. FIND the section(s) whose purpose is to demonstrate that the colonists had tried to work things out with the king.
Find passages that reveal or reflect an author's point of view or purpose, as well as passages that distinguish (or highlight similarities) between two separate points of view. (R.CCR.6)	• FIND a sentence that clarifies the author's position on this issue. • How does the author address conflicting viewpoints? FIND some examples. • How can we tell the author believes the theft was justified? FIND evidence.
Integrate and evaluate content that's presented in diverse media and formats, including visually and quantitatively, as well as in words. (R.CCR.7)	• FIND a picture that shows how the hungry caterpillar feels after Saturday's meal. • FIND a figure that expands on the information presented in paragraph 2. • Can you FIND any evidence for a regional trend in flu cases? Look in all three of the sources that were provided: map, data table, and CDC bulletin.
Identify the components, strengths, and weaknesses of an argument. (R.CCR.8)	• FIND two specific reasons that support the author's claim. • FIND a piece of evidence that isn't relevant to the author's argument.
Compare two or more texts and identify similarities/differences in content, focus, style, etc. (R.CCR.9)	• Read these creation myths. FIND some common elements. • FIND an idea that's present in both the main article and the sidebar. • FIND information in Source 1 that conflicts with Source 2. • FIND rhetorical features that are common to both texts.

Teacher Talk

- ➔ To simplify things for primary-grade students, English language learners, students with reading disabilities, or students who are new to the tool, you can use shorter, less complex text passages (read them aloud if needed), design multiple-choice tasks rather than open-ended ones (e.g., "Which two of the statements below support the author's claim?"), or have students hunt for items as a class or in groups rather than on their own.
- ➔ This tool can be used at multiple points in an instructional sequence. Use it for diagnostic purposes at the start of a unit/school year. (What do students know already?) Use it for formative assessment purposes in the middle of a unit/school year. (Which skills still need work?) Use it summatively to determine which skills students have mastered by the end of a unit/school year.
- ➔ When creating your tasks, think carefully about how long it will take students to read the required passages—particularly if you're working with beginning readers or students with learning disabilities. Be careful not to create more tasks than students can complete in the allotted time.
- ➔ Move beyond traditional printed texts; have students "hunt" in videos, audio clips, charts, etc.
- ➔ Since friendly competition can increase student engagement (Marzano, 2007), some teachers turn Scavenger Hunt into a game where students compete for points (one point for each correct item; the student/team that's first to find all items correctly gets three bonus points, second-to-finish gets two, etc.). Besides being fun for students, low-stakes games that target essential content have been linked to significant gains in learning and achievement (Haystead & Marzano, 2009).
- ➔ If students will hunt in teams rather than on their own, set things up so that all team members have a role to play. At the minimum, everyone should have to discuss and agree upon the final responses.
- ➔ While find-it tasks will have ties to individual reading standards, they won't always target those standards completely. (If a standard calls for students to *evaluate* a director's decision to make changes to an original script, for example, having students *find* those changes wouldn't be sufficient.) In these cases, you can target the standards more fully by posing appropriate follow-up questions during the discussion in Step 5. Here's what this might look like for Common Core Standard RL.8.7:
    - During the scavenger hunt, challenge students to *find* aspects of a live production that depart from the original script.
    - During the discussion, help students *evaluate* the director's decision to make those changes as called for by the standard. ("Why might the director have chosen to make these changes? What impact did they have? Do you feel the changes were good ones? Why or why not?")

  Note that in this example, it's the follow-up questions—not the original find-it task—that address the standard in question.
- ➔ While the focus of this tool is on finding text-based information and evidence, you can design hunts around other Common Core skills/standards as well. For example: Find a grammar error (L.CCR.1), or find at least three words that are too informal for this type of writing piece (L.CCR.3).

Name: Date:

Scavenger Hunt

Text(s) to search:

My task:

Here's where I found what I was looking for (include page, paragraph, or line number if appropriate):

Text(s) to search:

My task:

Here's where I found what I was looking for (include page, paragraph, or line number if appropriate):

Text(s) to search:

My task:

Here's where I found what I was looking for (include page, paragraph, or line number if appropriate):

Single-Sentence Summaries

What is it?

A tool that improves comprehension and develops summarizing skills (Common Core Reading Standards 10 and 2) by teaching students to sum up key points as they read

What are the benefits of using this tool?

There are many different strategies for improving reading comprehension. What we love about this one is its simplicity. (Students write a one-sentence summary for every paragraph they read.) Teaching students this simple strategy for constructing meaning from assigned texts has been found to facilitate comprehension and recall for both low- and high-ability readers (Doctorow, Wittrock, & Marks, 1978).

What are the basic steps?

1. Introduce and explain the value of the Single-Sentence Summaries technique. ("It's a technique that will help you better understand and remember what you read.")

2. Model the technique by generating a summary sentence (or picture) for each paragraph in an informational text. Think aloud as you work so that students can see what the process entails.

   Tip: Emphasize the idea that a summary sentence only has to capture the big idea (the main point the author is trying to convey); it doesn't have to reiterate every little fact and detail.

3. Practice the technique as a class before having students use it on their own. ("Let's review the sentences you came up with for this paragraph. Who wants to share first?")

4. Provide guidance and feedback as needed—remind students that a summary sentence should be shorter than the original passage, help them distinguish between big ideas that are important to include and smaller ones that aren't, etc If students are struggling, go back to Step 2.

5. Have students use the technique to take notes on specific reading assignments. Encourage them to revisit their notes as a means of reviewing and studying the big ideas.

6. Encourage students to use the technique independently—not just in your class and not just when you tell them to—by explaining that it can help them understand and remember material from *any* informational text passage.

How is this tool used in the classroom?

✔ To teach students a simple strategy for improving reading comprehension

✔ To develop students' summarizing skills

EXAMPLE : Secondary science

A science teacher asked students to summarize the information from a textbook section on the Earth's mantle using single sentences or sketches, whichever worked better to capture the essence of each paragraph. One student's work is shown below. Notice how she summarized the first paragraph using a sketch and the second using a sentence—and how in both cases, she focused on main ideas rather than minor details. Teaching students to eliminate the kinds of detailed facts and figures that often appear in science texts, but aren't critical to take away or memorize, was something her teacher had been working on for weeks.

> At the center of the Earth is a solid inner core, outside of which lies the liquid outer core. The **mantle** is the layer that lies directly above the outer core. It extends about 2900 kilometers below the surface of the Earth, and accounts for approximately 80 percent of Earth's volume and 68 percent of its mass.
>
> The density of the mantle increases with depth. A possible reason for this increase in density is the higher percentage of iron that is found in the lower mantle. Temperature is another factor that increases with depth. The upper mantle is around 870°C, while the lower mantle is around 2200°C.

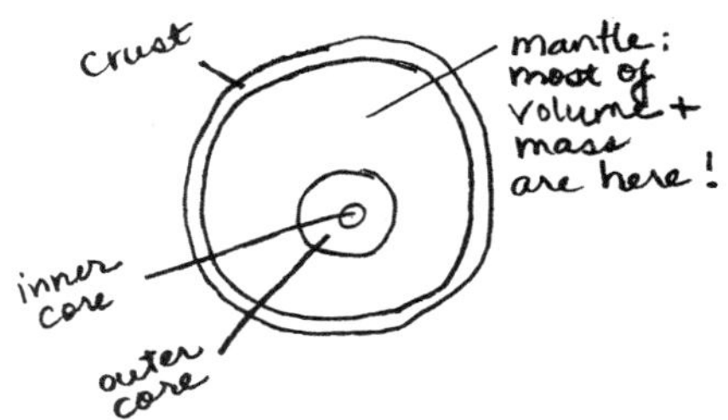

Density and temperature increase with depth.

Teacher Talk

➔ Prepare students for success with this tool—and with Common Core Reading Standard 2—by teaching them how to generate high-quality summary sentences. Here are some scaffolding tips:

- Help students understand the qualities of a successful summary sentence by creating a set of good and not-so-good examples for a specific text passage. Discuss why the good examples are good and what's wrong with the others (e.g., "focuses on a small detail rather than the main point" or "identifies the topic of the paragraph rather than the point the paragraph is making").
- Help students make smarter choices about what to include in their summary sentences by reviewing tips/strategies for identifying main ideas (several can be found in the Main Idea tool, pp. 33–36).
- Help students write on-target summary sentences by giving them two to four words that relate to the main idea of each paragraph and instructing them to build those words into their sentences.
- If students aren't ready to generate summary sentences on their own, give them three or four options to choose from (one that's a solid summary sentence, two or three that aren't). Have them pick the best one and explain their reasoning.
- Use summary sentences or paragraphs from well-written textbooks to show students how dense, detail-rich passages can be successfully condensed/reduced down to the important bits.

Structure, Function, Relationships

What is it?

A tool that has students analyze texts to determine the functions of (and relationships between) structural elements—stanzas, paragraphs, stage directions, etc.

What are the benefits of using this tool?

Common Core Reading Standard 5 asks students to explore the functions (and functional relationships) of structural elements within a text. This tool prepares students to conduct these kinds of analyses, both by familiarizing them with the ways that structural elements function within a text and by giving them the vocabulary they need to discuss these functions and relationships.

What are the basic steps?

1. Discuss the kinds of structural elements that students might be asked to analyze (e.g., sentence, paragraph, scene, sidebar). Confirm that students can define and locate examples of these elements.

2. Explain that these elements can have different functions within a text, and that students will often be asked to figure out what these functions are.

3. Use words from the Word Bank on p. 49 to familiarize students with some of these functions. Use concrete examples to define and illustrate the various functions (one at a time, not all at once!).

   Sample language: What does it mean to *introduce* something? Which paragraph in this text serves to introduce the author's main idea? Which paragraph in this story introduces the main character?

4. Develop questions that require students to identify the functions of (or relationships between) structural elements in a text and record them on the handout (p. 49). Use these frames to help you:
   - What is the function of Element X in this text/text passage?
   - How does Element X contribute to (or fit into) the overall structure?
   - How does Element X contribute to the development of ideas, meaning, plot, theme, or setting?
   - What is the connection or relationship between Element X and Element Y?

   Note: It's fine to develop questions that focus on multiple elements at once. For example, "How do paragraphs X, Y, and Z contribute to the overall structure of the story?"

5. Work through some of these questions as a class. Show students how to consult the Word Bank for ideas and use Word Bank terms in their responses when appropriate. For example:
   - What function does the opening sentence of this fairy tale serve? It *introduces* the setting.
   - How does the last section relate to the previous ones? It *summarizes* the ideas they contained.

6. Challenge students to tackle the remaining questions independently. Evaluate each response carefully, keeping in mind that students may generate different, but equally valid, responses than the ones you had in mind when you generated your questions.

7. Use students' responses to gauge their skill level. Provide additional instruction as needed.

How is this tool used in the classroom?

✔ To help students analyze the functions of/relationships between structural elements in a text

EXAMPLES: Sample questions representing different grade levels and text types are shown below, along with the corresponding answers. Word Bank terms have been italicized for emphasis.

Question	Response
What function does the fable's last sentence serve?	It *states* the lesson or moral.
What is the function of the underlined sentence within this narrative?	It *provides a transition between* the events being described in the first and second paragraphs.
How is paragraph 4 important to the development of the ideas in this biography?	Paragraph 4 *establishes* Robinson's moral objection to segregation, a theme that is revisited repeatedly throughout the rest of the biography.
What is the relationship between the first and last four lines in this stanza?	The last four lines *provide a contrast to* the first four. The first four note that it should be a time for celebration; the last four reveal the sadness of what has happened.

Teacher Talk

➔ You may want to use concrete objects rather than texts to introduce the idea that structural elements have specific functions. Start by showing students a familiar object like a water bottle. Ask them to identify its structural elements and describe the function of each (screw cap *lets you access the water*, flat bottom *lets it stand up*...). Then explain—and use examples to show—that the structural elements of a text, like the structural elements of an object, have specific functions.

➔ Clarify that the list of Word Bank terms won't cover every possible function or relationship—that students should use the list if it's helpful, but use their own words instead if they prefer.

➔ To target Common Core Reading Standard 7 as well as Reading Standard 5, add questions that address the function of visual or multimedia elements (illustrations, video clips, etc.). For example, "What does this illustration add to the text? It *emphasizes* and *adds to* the spookiness of the setting by..."

➔ To reduce ambiguity and provide practice for standardized tests, you can design multiple-choice items rather than free-response items in Step 4. You can create these items from scratch (see the box below for an example) or you can borrow existing ones, like Item 5 from this set of eleventh-grade sample items developed by the Partnership for Assessment of Readiness for College and Careers [PARCC]: http://www.parcconline.org/sites/parcc/files/Grade11SampleItems.pdf.

How does the highlighted section *most strongly* contribute to the text as a whole?

a) It *establishes* the colonists' beliefs about the purpose of government.

b) It *lists* specific grievances and violations of the colonists' rights.

c) It *provides evidence* to support the colonists' claim that asserting their independence is justified.

d) It *presents* the colonists' position that people are endowed by their Creator with certain unalienable rights.

Name: Date:

Structure, Function, Relationships

Question	Response (underline Word Bank terms if used)

Word Bank

adds to, addresses, advances, clarifies, compares, concludes, connects, contrasts, contradicts, defines, depicts, describes, develops, elaborates on, emphasizes, establishes, explains, identifies, illustrates, includes, introduces, lists, makes it easy to find, offers, presents/provides (an alternative to, a contrast to, a transition between, reasons for, evidence for), previews, reiterates, retells, states, strengthens, summarizes, supports, synthesizes, ties together, traces, wraps up

Writing Tools

We are all apprentices in a craft where no one ever becomes a master.

—Ernest Hemingway

Writing is the primary basis upon which your work, your learning, and your intellect will be judged—in college, in the workplace, and in the community.

—Marquette University website, "Writing Across the Curriculum"

David Conley is considered one of the leading experts on college readiness. So we take notice when he writes, "If we could institute only one change to make students more college ready, it should be to increase the amount and quality of writing students are expected to produce" (Conley, 2007, pp. 27–28).

The tools in this chapter were designed to help implement this "one change," both by engaging students in a range of writing tasks and by developing the writing skills associated with college and career success. Collectively, these tools prepare students to

- understand and produce the three types of writing highlighted in the Common Core State Standards: argument/opinion, informative/explanatory, and narrative;
- craft clear and coherent pieces that reflect task, purpose, and audience;
- evaluate source quality, and incorporate textual details and evidence into their writing; and
- see writing as an ongoing process that's enhanced through planning, revision, and collaboration with fellow writers.

These are the twelve tools that help students build this diverse skill set:

1. **Arguments: A TREAT to Write!** makes arguments easier for students to write by summarizing the must-have elements in an easy-to-remember acronym.
2. **As It Says in the Text...** teaches students specific phrases that they can use to incorporate textual details and evidence into their writing.
3. **Gallery Walk** engages students in learning and writing about critical content with the help of their classmates; the focus is on having students gather, summarize, and synthesize information from multiple sources.

4. **I Sense a Good Narrative** prepares students to write more vivid and engaging narratives by helping them include a variety of sensory details (sights, sounds, smells, etc.).

5. **Knee-to-Knee Conference** gives students the opportunity to listen to what they've written, discuss their work with a partner, and revise their drafts accordingly.

6. **Map It Out** prepares students to write higher-quality pieces by having them outline and organize their ideas using specially designed visual organizers. Twelve different organizers reflecting ten different writing types are provided for students' use.

7. **The Missing Links** teaches students how linking and organizing words can be used to improve the quality and clarity of their writing.

8. **RAFT** helps students understand that the content and style of their written work should reflect their **R**oles as writers, the **A**udiences they're writing for, the **F**ormats of their pieces, and the **T**opics (or tasks) they're addressing.

9. **Search Party** familiarizes students with the key components of arguments, informational pieces, and narratives by having them search for and examine these components in existing writing samples.

10. **Source Savvy** provides students with clear criteria for evaluating the quality and usefulness of potential sources.

11. **Stop, Read, Revise** trains students to read what they've written and work to improve it; specific criteria are provided to guide and focus the process.

12. **Writing Frames** presents a wealth of customizable writing frames that can be used to assess students' content knowledge, develop specific writing skills, and encourage regular writing.

Note: Although there isn't a specific tool for targeting Writing Standard 6, you can address this standard by having students use technology to produce, publish, and collaborate on their writing assignments. Simple possibilities include asking students to type, format, and revise their pieces using a word processing program; research their pieces on the Internet; or share their writing and request feedback via a class blog or website.

Arguments: A TREAT to Write!

What is it?

A tool that makes arguments easier for students to write by spelling out the critical components

What are the benefits of using this tool?

The Common Core Writing Standards are very clear about the components an argument should contain (see Standard 1). If we expect our students to achieve this standard, then, they must be equally clear about what these components are. This tool provides that clarity by summarizing the "must haves" in an easy-to-remember acronym. Referring to the acronym while planning and writing their pieces reminds students to include the essential elements in their drafts.

What are the basic steps?

1. Review the definition of a written argument (a piece where you make a claim and support it with reasons and evidence) and the kinds of prompts that signal one (e.g., "Take a position on…").
2. Explain that well-crafted arguments contain several critical components, and that students should include these components in their written (and spoken) arguments.
3. Show students how the acronym TREAT can help them remember the critical components:

   T*hesis:* State your claim/position.

   R*easons:* Give clear reasons to support your claim/position.

   E*vidence:* Support your reasons with relevant evidence (facts, details, observations, quotations).

   A*lternatives:* Address alternative claims/positions.

   T*ie it up:* Conclude with a sentence or section that follows from and sums up your argument.
4. Craft several argument pieces as a class using the acronym as a guide. Talk your way through the process so that students understand what each component entails.
5. Assign argument-writing tasks for practice. Remind students to refer to the acronym as they work.

   Tip: In the beginning especially, you may want to give students a list of reasons/evidence to use in their pieces. This will let them focus on their writing rather than on gathering these items themselves.
6. Remind students to use the acronym when working independently (e.g., on a standardized test).

How is this tool used in the classroom?

✔ To help students craft complete and quality arguments

Teacher Talk

➔ Modify the acronym to match the demands of Common Core Writing Standard 1 for your specific grade level. An elementary teacher might eliminate the "A" (since addressing Alternatives isn't required until seventh grade) and change the last "T" (Tie it up) to an "E" (End) to get the acronym TREE.

As It Says in the Text…

What is it?

A tool that helps students integrate text-based details/evidence into their speech and writing

What are the benefits of using this tool?

The Common Core State Standards require students to support their thinking with text-based details and evidence (see, for example, Writing Standard 9, Reading Standards 1 and 3, and Speaking & Listening Standard 4). Because this skill is new for many students, it's one that needs to be taught explicitly and practiced regularly. This tool familiarizes students with the kind of language that referring to texts requires. It gives them lead-in phrases that they can use to introduce textual material, and it encourages them to build those phrases into their speech and writing.

What are the basic steps?

1. Review the sentence stems/lead-in phrases on p. 56. Select a few to focus on (generate your own if you prefer), and post them in an easily visible location.
2. Leave the stems up so students can refer to them in class. Print copies of the selected stems (or all the stems) for students to use as a reference at home and in their other classes.
3. Review the stems with students. Show students how these kinds of phrases are used to introduce texts/textual material, both by highlighting their use in existing writing pieces and by using the stems yourself when discussing texts in class (point to the stems as you use them).
4. Give students practice using the selected stems by posing questions that require text-based answers. (Have all students record a response on paper; call on one or more students to share.) Remind students to refer to the text when answering by pointing to the list of stems.
5. Encourage students to use the stems during all text-based discussions. (Point to the list to remind them.) Getting students to use the stems independently will require regular and repeated practice.
6. Explain that students should use the stems in their writing as well as their speech. Assign writing tasks that require text-based responses, and give students feedback on their incorporation of the stems/text-based details.

How is this tool used in the classroom?

✔ To help students build textual details and evidence into their speaking and writing

EXAMPLE: Elementary

Here, a third grader used two different lead-in phrases (marked by arrows) to introduce information from an assigned text:

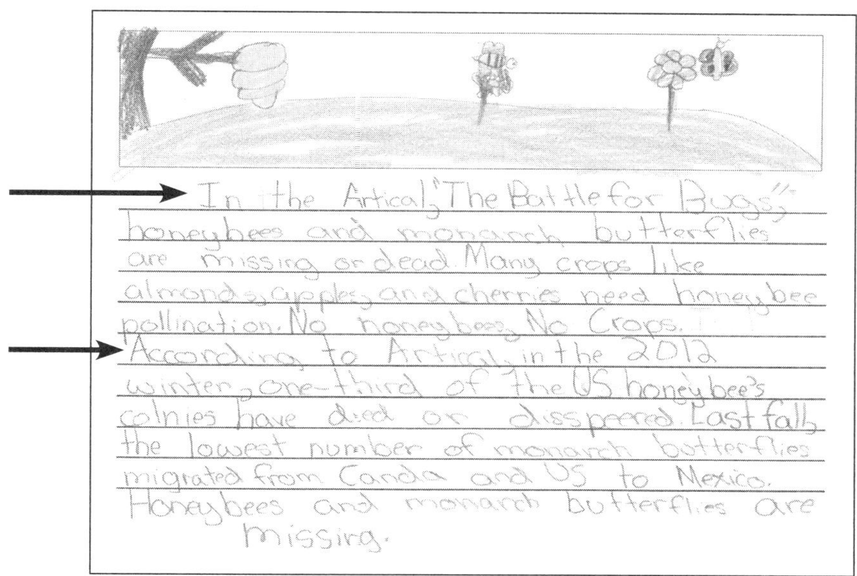

In the Artical, "The Battle for Bugs," honeybees and monarch butterflies are missing or dead. Many crops like almonds, apples, and cherries need honeybee pollination. No honeybees, No Crops. According to Artical, in the 2012 winter, one-third of the US honeybee's colnies have died or disspeared. Last fall, the lowest number of monarch butterflies migrated from Canda and US to Mexico. Honeybees and monarch butterflies are missing.

Teacher Talk

➔ Help students develop the vocabulary they need to refer to sources properly by discussing terms that they can use to refer to parts of a source (e.g., stanza, line, sidebar, paragraph) as well as options for referring to sources as a whole. ("With a set of numbered sources, you can refer to a source by its title or you can refer to it by number—for example, 'Source 1.'")

➔ Clarify that providing details/evidence from a text can involve paraphrasing or quoting directly. Discuss the difference between these two options, and teach students how to format and punctuate each one (e.g., Are quotation marks needed? Do end-punctuation marks go inside or outside?).

Note: You may also want to distinguish paraphrasing and quoting from *plagiarizing* (supports Common Core Writing Standard 8). Using concrete examples can help students grasp the difference.

➔ Because the Common Core State Standards expect students to analyze and use information from different types of sources (W.CCR.8, R.CCR.7, SL.CCR.2), it's important to show students how lead-in phrases can be used to reference material from figures, videos, audio clips, etc.

➔ Teach students to recognize test questions/prompts that require including text-based (or other source-based) details in their responses by familiarizing them with tip-off words like "provide evidence from the text" or "support your response with specific details from the various sources."

➔ To up the level of difficulty and address additional standards (Common Core R.CCR.9 and W.CCR.8), design tasks that require integrating information from multiple sources.

Name: Date:

Lead-In Phrases

In source X, ______. In chapter X, ______. In paragraph X, ______. In line X, ______.

In source X by author X, it says ______.

From source X, we learn that ______.

At the beginning/end of source X (or chapter X), ______.

On page X, person X (or character X) says/does ______.

On page X, for example, ______.

Source X (or author X) describes/contends/contradicts/explains/concludes/supports ______.

According to source X, ______.

According to person X (author or other individual mentioned in the text), ______.

As it says on page X, ______. As it says in paragraph X, ______. As it says in source X, ______.

As noted/stated in the text, ______.

As noted/reported by person X, ______.

Person X, an expert in ______, noted that ______. Person X, ______ (job title), noted that ______.

Sources X and Y both ______.

Source X contradicts source Y in that ______.

According to the data in Figure/Table X, ______.

As seen/shown in the figure on page X, ______. ("Figure" can refer to a chart, map, picture, or other visual.)

Gallery Walk

What is it?

An interactive and collaborative learning tool that has students use a variety of sources, both print and digital, to learn and write about critical content

What are the benefits of using this tool?

In recent years, museums have started using interactive, multimedia exhibits to make learning more meaningful, memorable, and fun for visitors. So why not do the same in our classrooms? During a Gallery Walk, students acquire information about a selected topic by viewing a series of "exhibits" and summarizing key points with their classmates. Besides giving students a much-needed break from sitting still and listening, the Gallery Walk format supports a number of Common Core Standards by requiring students to discuss, summarize, and synthesize information from a variety of different sources.

What are the basic steps?

1. Prepare for a Gallery Walk lesson as follows:
   - Divide your content into four to eight meaningful chunks (one topic or theme per chunk). Each chunk of information will be presented at a different exhibit in your gallery.
   - Give each chunk of information a descriptive title (Famous Women Scientists, Famous Women Authors, etc.). These titles will become the titles of your gallery exhibits.
   - Record the name of your gallery (e.g., Famous Women in American History) and a question for students to think about as they view the gallery (optional) on the Gallery Notes handout (p. 61).
   - Brainstorm a list of items/documents you could use to present the content to students—news clippings, images, graphs, audio files, manipulatives, poems, etc. Be creative and aim for variety.
   - Decide which items to include at each exhibit, and make a list of what goes where (e.g., Exhibit 2 is a collection of WWII photos). Arrange the exhibits accordingly on the day of the actual lesson.
2. Divide students into groups, and assign each group to a different starting exhibit. Tell students how much time they'll have to examine each exhibit, and alert them when it's time to switch. Numbering the exhibits in advance will help students know where to go when you call time.
3. Ask students to record the four most important facts/ideas from each exhibit on their handouts.
4. Instruct group members to share and explain their choices, come to a consensus about which points are the most important, and revise their notes as needed. Taking notes in pencil will help.
5. Assign a writing task that requires students to summarize and synthesize what they learned from the exhibits. (If students got a focus question in Step 1, they should respond to that as well.) Students can outline their pieces as a team (this offers support to developing writers) or on their own.
6. Teach students to incorporate specific facts and details from the exhibits into their drafts (e.g., "The photo from Exhibit 2 shows..."). The As It Says in the Text tool (pp. 54–56) can help.

How is this tool used in the classroom?

✔ To present critical content in an engaging and interactive way

✔ To develop key research and writing skills, including using multiple sources

✔ To engage students in collaborative conversations about selected topics and texts

EXAMPLE 1: Primary science

A kindergarten teacher created a "four seasons gallery" to help students see how different things (weather, plants, animals, people) are affected by the seasons. To make the Gallery Walk format more age appropriate, she created "pictures only" exhibits and replaced the standard Gallery Notes handout with a visual organizer like the one at the right (students sketched what they learned from each exhibit on the organizer).

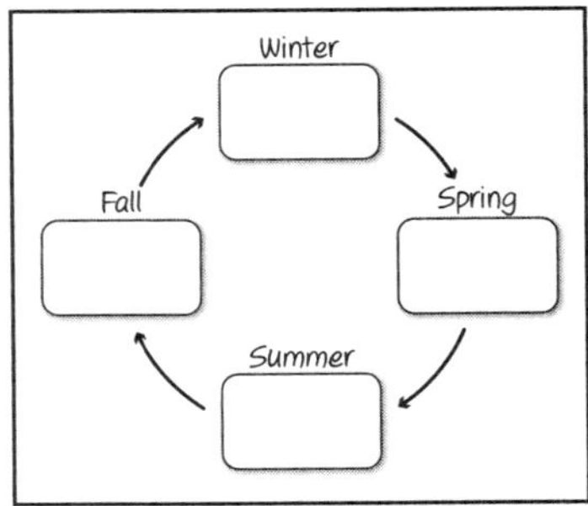

EXAMPLE 2: Secondary history

A history teacher used the Gallery Walk format to introduce a unit on the 1920s. He set up themed exhibits on key topics, including music, women's rights and roles, and Prohibition—and he used a variety of artifacts to help students get a feel for the decade (see below for a partial list).

- Newspaper headlines and advertisements from the time period
- Clips from Ken Burns's documentary, *Jazz*
- Images of women from the turn of the century and from the 1920s
- Copies of the 18th and 19th Amendments to the US Constitution
- Graphs/data reflecting the growth of specific industries, particularly the automobile industry
- Excerpts from *The Great Gatsby* and *A Cultural History of the United States Through the Decades*

When the gallery closed (it was left open for a week), students summarized what they had learned by writing illustrated reports about the 1920s. In their reports, they addressed the focus question they had been asked to think about: Why might the 1920s be referred to as the "Roaring" Twenties?

EXAMPLE 3: Elementary science

A third-grade teacher set up the four stations described below to develop students' understanding of magnets (part of a unit addressing Next Generation Science Standard 3-PS2-3).

- Station 1 had students test the magnetic properties of different items, put them into magnetic and nonmagnetic groups, and describe the interactions between magnetic and nonmagnetic items.
- Station 2 had students explore the effects of orientation and distance on magnetic forces.
- Station 3 presented pictures showing how magnets are used in the workplace and everyday life.
- Station 4 was a look-and-listen station with a short video presentation on magnets.

After working in teams to summarize four important things that they had learned about magnets (one from each station), students shared and compared ideas as a class. They then used their combined knowledge to create an illustrated class book titled *What We Know About Magnets*.

EXAMPLE 4: Secondary art

An art teacher used the Gallery Walk format instead of his usual lecture to introduce students to Impressionism. The exhibits he developed are described in the box below.

- Exhibit 1 contained a list of Impressionist painting techniques and characteristics.
- Exhibit 2 featured encyclopedia articles on Impressionism.
- Exhibit 3 displayed the kind of art valued by the Académie des Beaux-Arts, which dominated the French art scene prior to the advent of Impressionism and rejected the work of the early Impressionists.
- Exhibit 4 presented a translation of Louis Leroy's scathing review "The Exhibition of the Impressionists" from the French newspaper *Le Charivari.*
- Exhibit 5 featured dossiers on individual painters containing brief biographical sketches as well as reproductions of their most famous pieces.

When the gallery closed, students demonstrated what they had learned by choosing a painting from one of the dossiers and explaining how it both reflected the Impressionist style and differed from earlier styles of painting. Students were required to refer to information from at least three different exhibits in their explanations.

Variation 1: Student-Designed Gallery

This variation, which supports Common Core Writing Standard 7, encourages collaborative research by having teams of students (rather than the teacher) develop the gallery exhibits. To use it, divide the content into chunks, and assign each chunk to a different team of students. Instruct each team to research its assigned topic, gather appropriate exhibit materials, and assemble an engaging and informative exhibit. Let teams know what date the gallery will open so that they can establish a timeline for completing their work. Offer assistance as needed throughout the project.

Variation 2: Opening-Day Gallery

This variation is used at the start of a semester or school year, both to spark students' interest in what they'll be learning and to assess students' prior knowledge. To use it, develop engaging exhibits that correspond to upcoming units in your curriculum. (A physical education teacher, for example, might create exhibits on the benefits of physical activity, various training and conditioning practices, fitness resources in the community, and injury prevention/safety.) Challenge students to guess the topic of each exhibit and list everything they know about that topic on a piece of paper. Collect the lists to see what students already know about the topics you plan to cover, and plan your instruction accordingly.

Teacher Talk

➔ Have students who don't get excited about (or thrive in) the traditional lecture environment? The interactive, collaborative, and get-out-of-your-seat nature of a Gallery Walk (combined with its use of digital resources) may be just what you need to get them engaged.

➔ An "exhibit" doesn't have to be anything fancy—objects on a table, maps on a bulletin board, a document on a desk, and a listening station with headphones would all count as exhibits. Do, however, vary the types of sources you give students to work with (include both print and digital).

➔ There's no "correct" way to divide your material into chunks (Step 1). If you were developing a Famous Women in American History gallery, for example, you could divide the material by time period (each exhibit would showcase women from a different decade), by occupation (one exhibit for scientists, one for artists, etc.), or by the women themselves (one exhibit per woman).

➔ Prepare students to have productive conversations (a focus of Common Core SL.CCR.1) by discussing rules and roles in advance—take turns speaking, be open to everyone's ideas, etc. Clarify that all students are expected to contribute—no sitting back and letting others do the work!

➔ To succeed with this tool, and with Common Core Writing Standard 8, students must know how to integrate information from outside sources into their work without plagiarizing, and how to cite their sources properly. Teach and model these skills until students are comfortable with them.

➔ Many teachers use the Gallery Walk format to prepare students for the kinds of document-based essay/research questions that are increasingly prevalent on standardized exams. Why? Because the interactive and collaborative nature of a Gallery Walk scaffolds and makes practicing these kinds of writing tasks more fun. (Having students take notes, outline their pieces, and look for supporting details in the provided documents as a team is a great way to scaffold the thinking and writing process.) To use the tool for this purpose, be sure to give students a writing prompt or question to think about as they view the exhibits (as the tool is written, this step is optional), and have them use this prompt/question to focus the note-taking and writing processes.

Note: Document-based questions (and accompanying supporting documents) are readily available online if you don't have time to generate your own. Quality varies, though, so be selective!

➔ The beauty of a Gallery Walk is that it lets you teach your content and engage your students while building a number of Common Core skills, including identifying and summarizing key ideas (R.CCR.2), discussing content collaboratively (SL.CCR.1), gathering and integrating information from a variety of sources (R.CCR.7, W.CCR.7–8, SL.CCR.2), and supporting conclusions with source-based details (R.CCR.1, W.CCR.9). To target additional skills/standards, simply design your focus question or synthesis task around the standard(s) of your choice. A task that requires students to compare multiple accounts of the same event, for example, would support Informational Reading Standard 9.

➔ Want to add a technology connection? Use QR codes (print one per station) to help students visit interesting places (e.g., Stonehenge, a Civil War battlefield, the American Museum of Natural History) or view other online resources via a mobile device. The codes are easy to create using a site like www.QRstuff.com. Another option is to make one of your exhibits a computer station where students can search for additional information about the topic at hand.

Name: ____________________ Date: ____________________

Gallery Notes

Gallery topic:

Question to think about or summary task to complete:

Members of my group:

Exhibit: ______________________________

(Record the name of the exhibit here. Use a different notes sheet for each exhibit.)

Most important ideas:

1.

2.

3.

4.

I Sense a Good Narrative

What is it?

A tool that prepares students to craft more vivid and interesting narratives by encouraging them to include a variety of sensory details

What are the benefits of using this tool?

Gifted narrative writers are experts at using sensory language to make their writing come alive. This tool helps all students develop this critical skill by encouraging them to jot down possible sights, sounds, smells, tastes, and sensations at the outset of the writing process. ("Picture the event you're going to be writing about in your mind. What do you see? Hear? Smell? Taste? Feel?") Engaging students in this kind of pre-writing task targets both Common Core Writing Standard 3, which addresses the importance of sensory language specifically, and Writing Standard 5, which focuses on strengthening writing via planning.

What are the basic steps?

1. Use specific text passages to illustrate the way that writers use sensory details to make their pieces come alive. ("How does Longfellow bring Paul Revere's ride to life in this poem? What kinds of details does he provide? What specifically do his words help us see, hear, and feel?")
2. Have students search these passages for specific *see*, *smell*, *taste*, *touch*, and *hear* words (e.g., "the sound of arms, and the tramp of feet" or "felt the damp of the river fog"). Discuss the effect that these words have on the overall success of the piece.
3. Talk to students about the importance of including key sensory details in their own writing. Show them how the I Sense a Good Narrative organizer on p. 64 can help them map out these details in advance.
4. Complete an organizer as a class using a topic/event that students are familiar with. ("If we were writing about our field trip to the county fair, what might we put in the *see* box? The *smell* box?") Fill in as many boxes as you can.
5. Have students use the class-completed organizer to draft their own narratives about the selected topic or event. Remind students to build the details from the organizer into their drafts.
6. Distribute blank organizers the next time you assign a narrative writing task. Instruct students to complete the organizer before they begin writing and to incorporate the sensory details from their completed organizers into their drafts.

How is this tool used in the classroom?

✔ To help students craft more descriptive and vivid narratives

✔ To help students strengthen their writing via planning

EXAMPLE 1: Excerpt from a student's account of a big basketball game

I felt what seemed like a never-ending stream of sweat dripping from my forehead and millions of butterflies flapping around in my stomach. The opposing team's fans stomped their feet, waved their white towels, and did everything in their collective power to make me miss that fateful shot.

> Key words from this student's pre-writing organizer:
> See: *white towels* Hear: *feet stomping* Feel: *sweat on my face, butterflies in my stomach*

EXAMPLE 2: Excerpt from a student's "monster story"

When she felt the ground go thump thump thump, she knew it was time to run. She tried not to look back, but her fear got the better of her. And then she saw him...towering over her and blotting out the sun like a giant skyscraper.

> Key words from this student's pre-writing organizer:
> Feel: ground thumping, fear See: giant monster towering over her, darkness as he blots out the sun

EXAMPLE 3: Excerpt from a student's account of a scientific investigation

The bacteria we inoculated our media with had grown much more quickly than we had predicted! When we took the flask out of the shaker, the bacteria had grown so much that the liquid inside was now a cloudy yellow color — much more opaque than when we had put it in the night before. It was warm to the touch and had a pungent, very unpleasant smell that our teacher said was typical of E. coli bacteria. Our next step was to figure out...

> Key words from this student's pre-writing organizer:
> See: cloudy yellow color, opaque Feel: warm to the touch Smell: not so pleasant!!!

Teacher Talk

➔ Teaching students to jot down snippets of dialogue in the *hear* box will remind them to build dialogue into their narratives (a goal of Common Core Writing Standard 3).

➔ Don't assume this tool is only for English teachers! The Common Core ELA/Literacy Standards remind us that narrative writing has a place in other content areas as well. The ability to communicate precise descriptions of one's observations and findings (what was seen, heard, felt, etc.) is also a critical one for budding scientists to develop (National Research Council, 2012).

➔ Encourage students to include descriptive adjectives and adverbs (e.g., "sickly sweet, bubble gum-pink cotton candy" rather than "cotton candy") when completing their organizers and/or drafting their pieces. When appropriate, encourage students to incorporate figurative language as well (check out the simile in Example 2 above).

Name: Date:

I Sense a Good Narrative

TOPIC/EVENT you'll be writing about:

What do you SEE?

What do you HEAR?

What do you TASTE?

What do you FEEL?

What do you SMELL?

Knee-to-Knee Conference

What is it?

A tool that supports the Common Core's call for students to revise and strengthen their writing with help from their peers (Writing Standard 5) by having them listen to and discuss each other's drafts

What are the benefits of using this tool?

What's the advantage of hearing your own writing read to you? Well, as one second grader recently told us, "You can hear where it sounds 'scratchy' and where it doesn't make sense." We couldn't have said it better ourselves! Yet most students never get the chance to hear what they've written. This tool changes that by giving them a forum where they can listen to their drafts, evaluate the quality of their ideas, and identify any "scratchy" areas that need attention. It also reinforces the notion that revision is an essential part of the writing process, and that good writers take time to rethink and improve their work.

What are the basic steps?

1. Assign a writing task. Tell students to skip lines so that their work will be easier to read and edit.
2. Pair students up to read and listen to each other's drafts. Instruct them to
   - Read both drafts to themselves.
   - Read their partners' drafts aloud (slowly, so that their partners can really hear their writing).
   - Listen to their own drafts being read and think about things they might want to change.
3. Have students review and discuss their drafts. Use questions like the ones below (customize them to fit the writing task, then post or distribute copies) to spark and focus their conversations.
   - Which parts of the piece are clear? Which are hard to follow?
   - Do the ideas make sense? Are they in the best order?
   - What are the piece's greatest strengths? How could it be improved?

   Note: If you prefer, you can have students use The Seven Cs (a list of quality criteria for writing assignments, see p. 91) instead of discussion questions like the ones above to focus their conversations.
4. Instruct students to use what they learn to revise and improve their drafts.

How is this tool used in the classroom?

✔ To help students assess and improve the quality of their writing

✔ To engage students in collaborative conversations that involve giving and getting feedback

Teacher Talk

➔ This tool provides an opportunity to teach, model, and have students practice the "productive conversation behaviors" identified in Common Core Speaking & Listening Standard 1—behaviors like listening carefully, expressing ideas clearly, and responding to what others have said.

Map It Out

What is it?

A tool that helps students draft higher-quality arguments, explanatory pieces, and stories (Common Core Writing Standards 1–3) by teaching them to map out their ideas on visual organizers; using the organizers in this way supports the planning component of Common Core Writing Standard 5

What are the benefits of using this tool?

The value of mapping out our ideas before writing or speaking is one that everyone can appreciate—and one we need to instill in our students. Because students often struggle with traditional outlines (or worse, find them boring!), it's important to familiarize them with other outlining strategies. This tool teaches students how visual organizers can be used as outlining tools. The graphical format of these organizers makes them appealing to many students. It also promotes high-quality work by helping students visualize the structure of the pieces they're trying to write, as well as the individual elements those pieces should contain (e.g., claim, reasons, and conclusion in the case of a basic argument).

What are the basic steps?

1. Select a writing type to focus on (e.g., argument, story, comparison) and a visual organizer that matches it. See p. 67 for options, or create an organizer from scratch.
2. Use the organizer to teach (or remind students of) the elements that this writing type requires. Show them how the organizer contains "slots" for all the essential components. ("See how this argument organizer has slots for recording a claim, reasons, evidence, and a conclusion?")
3. Present a writing task that fits the organizer type you just reviewed. Show students how to use the organizer to outline a response (explain your thinking as you fill in the boxes). Then show them how you would use the completed organizer to help you structure and organize a first draft (write it out).
4. Call students' attention to the words/strategies you used to connect the ideas from your organizer.

   Tip: Prepare students to connect their ideas in a similarly smooth and organized way by reviewing the kinds of linking and organizing words that characterize this particular kind of writing piece (e.g., *first*, *next*, and *then* for a sequence piece). See The Missing Links, pp. 74–77, for assistance.
5. Give students a new writing task (same type), and have them map out their ideas on an organizer. Check their organizers *before* they start drafting their pieces so you can help them address any issues or deficiencies. (Have they sketched out the required elements? Are their ideas sound?)
6. Have students use their completed organizers to help them draft a response to the assigned task.
7. Review students' drafts. (Do they reflect students' outlines? Are all the components present? Did students use linking/organizing words to connect their ideas logically? Are there overall quality issues?) Provide feedback, and have students use that feedback to revise and improve their work.

How is this tool used in the classroom?

- ✔ To show students how visual organizers can be used as outlining tools
- ✔ To familiarize students with the key elements and requirements of specific writing types
- ✔ To promote high-quality writing by teaching students to plan out and revise their drafts

Teachers use this tool's visual organizers to help their students outline many different kinds of writing pieces—stories, arguments, comparison pieces, etc. In total, twelve different organizers reflecting ten different writing types are available (see box below for a list). All are available for download (www.ThoughtfulClassroom.com/Tools); three are shown in the text (pp. 71–73).

Note: Because the required elements for a given writing type will vary by grade level (consult your writing standards for specifics), you should feel free to modify the organizers before using them.

Available Organizers

Argument/Opinion Organizer (three versions available: beginning, intermediate, advanced)—Use this type of organizer to help students map out the basic components of an argument/opinion piece. Select the version whose structure most closely reflects the requirements for argument/opinion writing at your particular grade level.

Main Idea Organizer—Use this organizer to help students map out pieces that have a clear main idea and set of supporting details.

Topic-Subtopic Organizer—Use this organizer to help students map out informative/explanatory pieces about topics that have clear subtopics or subdivisions. Each subtopic becomes its own section in the final piece.

Matrix Organizer—This type of organizer is similar to a Topic-Subtopic Organizer; the main difference is that it's used for pieces that discuss two or more topics/items rather than one. Specifically, it helps students map out informative/explanatory pieces that address the same subtopics, features, or focus questions when discussing or comparing multiple items.

Comparison Organizer—Use this organizer to help students map out informative/explanatory pieces whose purpose is to compare two or more items.

Sequence Organizer—Use this organizer to help students map out informative/explanatory pieces whose purpose is to describe a sequence of steps, stages, or events.

Cycle Organizer—This organizer is similar to a Sequence Organizer; the difference is that it's used to map out pieces that discuss a cyclical (repeating) sequence of steps/stages/events rather than a linear one.

Cause-Effect Organizer—Use this organizer to help students map out informative/explanatory pieces whose purpose is to discuss the causes and/or effects of a specific issue, event, or other item.

Problem-Solution Organizer—Use this organizer to help students map out informative/explanatory pieces whose purpose is to present possible solutions for a specific problem.

Story Map—Use this organizer to help students plan out the key elements of a story before they actually write it.

EXAMPLE 1: Elementary (modeling example)

The organizer and paragraph that a fourth-grade teacher used to model the outlining and writing process for his students (Step 3) are shown below. Notice the clear correspondence between the information on his organizer and the information in his final piece (the content, as well as the way that it's structured). Notice also that he helped his students see how he had connected the ideas on his organizer (Step 4) by underlining the linking and organizing words in his final piece.

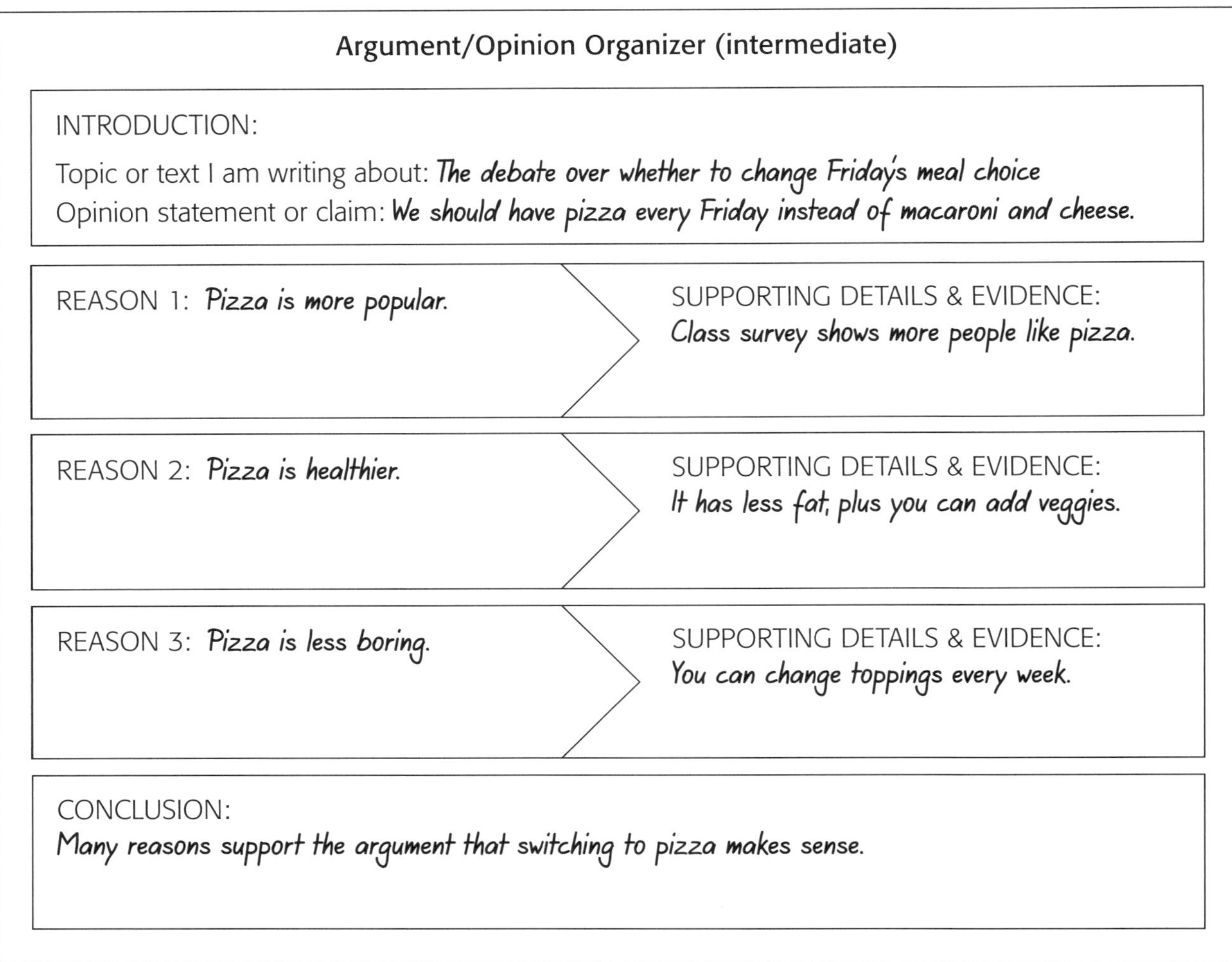

Argument/Opinion Organizer (intermediate)

INTRODUCTION:

Topic or text I am writing about: *The debate over whether to change Friday's meal choice*

Opinion statement or claim: *We should have pizza every Friday instead of macaroni and cheese.*

REASON 1: *Pizza is more popular.*	SUPPORTING DETAILS & EVIDENCE: *Class survey shows more people like pizza.*
REASON 2: *Pizza is healthier.*	SUPPORTING DETAILS & EVIDENCE: *It has less fat, plus you can add veggies.*
REASON 3: *Pizza is less boring.*	SUPPORTING DETAILS & EVIDENCE: *You can change toppings every week.*

CONCLUSION:

Many reasons support the argument that switching to pizza makes sense.

The Great Macaroni and Cheese Debate

Our school is currently debating some changes to the cafeteria menu, such as whether to continue serving macaroni and cheese every Friday. I believe that we should have pizza every Friday instead of macaroni and cheese. In the first place, pizza seems to be more popular among students. A survey of the class showed that more than half the people prefer pizza to macaroni and cheese. Second of all, pizza is a healthier option. Besides having less fat, it allows you to add vegetables in the form of toppings. Finally, students would be less likely to get bored of pizza since the toppings can be changed every week. Different toppings would make it feel like you were getting an entirely different food instead of the same thing every Friday! Taken together, these reasons support the argument that switching to pizza is a better option than sticking with macaroni and cheese.

EXAMPLE 2: Primary

Although the Common Core Writing Standards don't require providing supporting details in an argument/opinion piece until fourth grade, a first-grade teacher uses intermediate-level Argument/Opinion Organizers to develop this skill much earlier. Unlike the beginning-level organizers, which she uses at the start of the year, the intermediate ones have slots for including supporting details and evidence.

The organizers that two of her students completed in preparation for a writing assignment on bedtimes are shown below—one presents an argument in favor of bedtimes, the other against.

Argument/Opinion Organizer (intermediate)

INTRODUCTION

Topic/text I am writing about: bedtime

Opinion statement or claim: Yes I belive I should have a bedtime.

REASON 1 You could get sick.	SUPPORTING DETAILS/EVIDENCE I missed school when I didn't get that much sleep
REASON 2 You can get cranky.	SUPPORTING DETAILS/EVIDENCE People may not want to be by you.
REASON 3 You could fall asleep at school.	SUPPORTING DETAILS/EVIDENCE miss some important things.

CONCLUSION

It's important to have a bedtime.

Argument/Opinion Organizer (intermediate)

INTRODUCTION

Topic/text I am writing about: Bedtime

Opinion statement or claim: I think I shoudent have a bedtime.

REASON 1 I could fall asleep by myself	SUPPORTING DETAILS/EVIDENCE I have fallen asleep by myself befor
REASON 2 eat snaks and watch tv	SUPPORTING DETAILS/EVIDENCE you mihgtengoy it
REASON 3 Sleep dering the day	SUPPORTING DETAILS/EVIDENCE I took a long nap in the day

CONCLUSION

Thats why you shoadent have a bedtime

Teacher Talk

- ➔ This tool trains students to develop and strengthen their written work via planning, revising, and rewriting. In this regard, it's a perfect match for Common Core Writing Standard 5. To target Writing Standard 6 as well, have students write, illustrate, and/or collaborate on their pieces via computer (all three of these things can be done using Google Docs, for example).

- ➔ A scaffolding option for younger students or students who are new to the tool involves focusing on one element at a time (mapping *or* writing, rather than both). You might, for example, give students a completed organizer or create one as a class rather than having students complete their own—and then have students use the completed organizer to write their pieces.

- ➔ Emphasize the idea that if students take the time to make an organizer, it'll be that much easier for them to write a first draft—and they'll end up with pieces that are more complete and better organized as a result. ("If you've outlined your ideas on an organizer, all you'll need to do is flesh them out a bit and connect them together in a logical and orderly way using transition words.") Illustrate this point using concrete examples like the one on p. 68.

- ➔ It's important to use the organizers regularly so that students internalize the components and structure of the different writing types. Instruct students to picture the organizers and use them as guides even if the organizers aren't available (e.g., in a standardized testing situation).

- ➔ Before discussing the components of a particular type of piece (Step 2), review its overall purpose. ("Today we're going to be writing a comparison piece. The goal of this kind of piece is to highlight similarities and/or differences between whatever you've been asked to compare.") Making students aware that different pieces have different purposes, and that the purpose of a piece affects the way that it's written (content/structure/style), both complements the goals of Common Core Reading Standard 6 and facilitates better writing.

- ➔ In the beginning, have students write about topics they're familiar with, or provide them with the factual information they'd need to write their pieces (e.g., a list of reasons for/against something if they were writing an argument piece). Since the goal is to have students practice using the organizers, you don't want a lack of content knowledge to get in the way.

- ➔ If the goal is to help students develop high-quality pieces, you need to do more than teach them what elements to include; you need to teach them what those elements (and their pieces as a whole) should look like. At the minimum, review the criteria set out by the Common Core Writing Standards for your particular grade level and discuss those criteria with students. ("What should the introduction of an explanatory piece do?" "What kind of language makes for a great narrative?") Reviewing examples of high-quality work is another great way to help students understand and internalize the characteristics of quality.

- ➔ No time for students to fill in an organizer? Teach them to construct a checklist (mental or physical) of the required elements, and have them review their drafts to ensure that those elements are present.

Name: ______________________ Date: ______________

Argument/Opinion Organizer (intermediate)

INTRODUCTION:

Topic or text I am writing about:

Opinion statement or claim:

REASON 1:	SUPPORTING DETAILS & EVIDENCE:
REASON 2:	SUPPORTING DETAILS & EVIDENCE:
REASON 3:	SUPPORTING DETAILS & EVIDENCE:

CONCLUSION:

Name: Date:

Topic-Subtopic Organizer

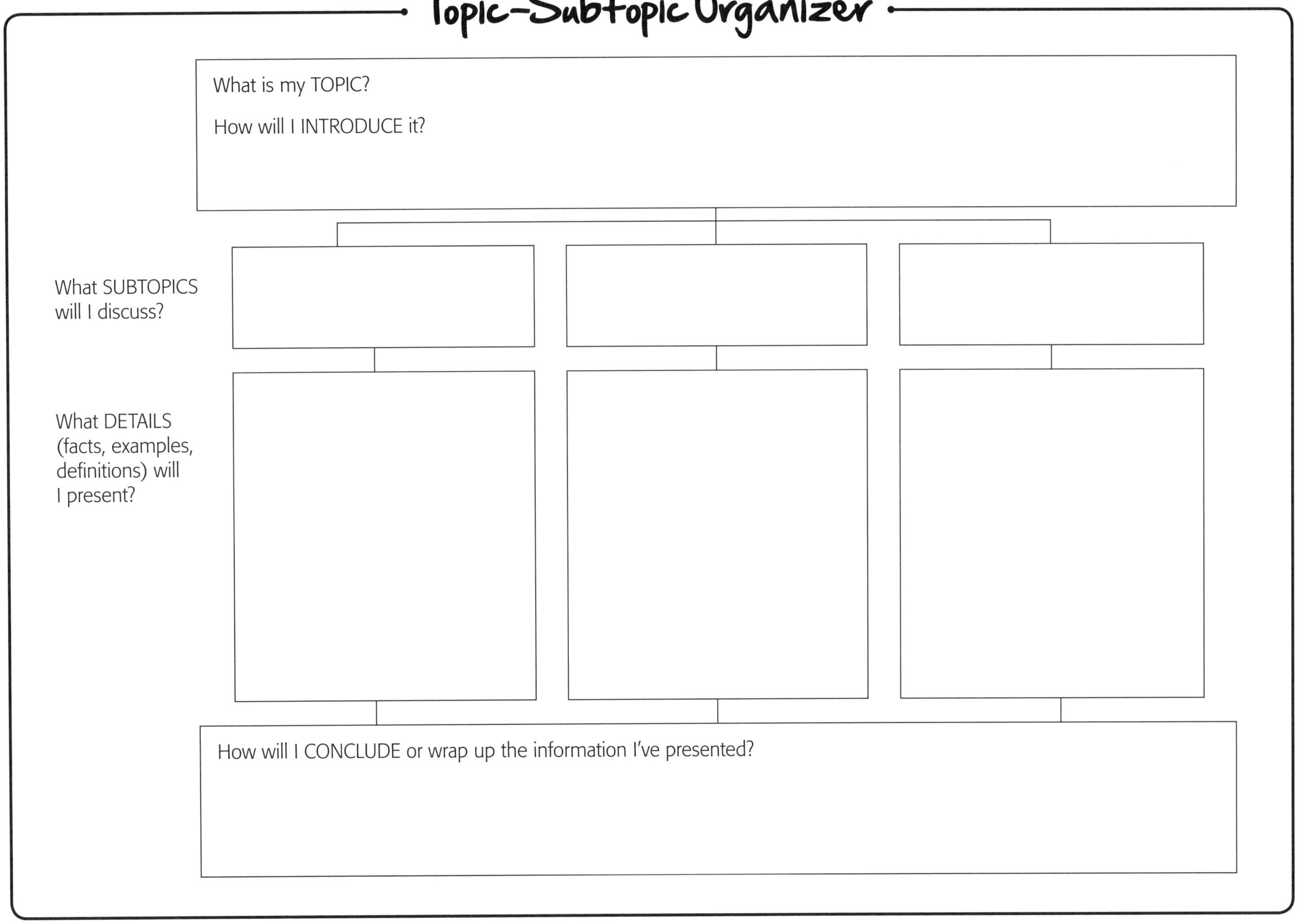

Name: Date:

Story Map

Who are the MAIN CHARACTERS? Briefly describe them.

What is the SETTING? Describe *where* and *when* the story takes place.

What is the PROBLEM or conflict?

How does the problem or conflict get resolved? (RESOLUTION)

What is the sequence of EVENTS? (First, next, then…)

The Missing Links

What is it?

A tool that familiarizes students with the kinds of linking words that good writers (and speakers) use to connect and organize their ideas

What are the benefits of using this tool?

Have you ever had trouble following the logic or sequence of a student's writing? In many cases, a lack of appropriate linking words is to blame. This tool helps students avoid these "missing links" by introducing them to the kinds of linking and organizing words that expert writers use to connect their ideas, and by encouraging them to include these words in their own work. Because the appropriate use of linking words is a requirement for all three Common Core writing types (opinion/argument, informative/explanatory, narrative), this tool has the power to improve student performance with regard to Writing Standards 1, 2, and 3.

What are the basic steps?

1. Create a word wall of commonly used linking and organizing words. See p. 77 for a list of options.

   Tip: Select words that are both age appropriate and appropriate for the type(s) of writing task(s) you'll be assigning (e.g., *first*, *next*, and *finally* would be good words for describing a series of steps or events).

2. Make a handout of your word-wall terms so students can refer to them when working at home or in other classes. If you prefer, you can distribute the entire list of terms from p. 77.

3. Review your word-wall terms with students.

4. Use a variety of writing samples to help students see how the kinds of linking and organizing words that you've selected can affect a piece's clarity, logic, organization, and flow. Use questions like these to guide the conversation:
   - What's the function of the word *first* in the opening paragraph of this particular writing sample? How does it help us as readers?
   - How does the writer of this piece connect his first two points? What words does he use? Why?
   - Does the writer's use of linking and organizing words affect our ability to follow his argument? If so, how?

5. Remind students to use words from the word wall (or the corresponding handout) when completing assigned writing tasks. Have them underline their word-wall terms for easy finding.

6. Give students specific feedback about their use of the word-wall terms and the impact of those terms on the quality and clarity of their writing.

How is this tool used in the classroom?

✔ To improve the organization, logic, and flow of students' writing

✔ To help students connect and communicate their ideas in a clear and orderly way

EXAMPLE: Elementary

The writing sample below, which was created in an elementary ESL classroom, shows how teaching (and having students practice using) linking and organizing words can help students begin to produce the kind of logically organized and well-structured pieces that the Common Core Writing Standards require.

Note the nice blend of order words (*first of all, second of all, finally*), contrasting-idea words (*however, but*), additional-point words (*also, and*), and a "here's my conclusion" word (*so*).

ESL

How To Convince My Dad To Buy Me A dog

I always wanted a dog, however my parents didn't, but I need it,
First of all, I would like to play soccer with the dog and I'll will love it.

Second of all, many people have dogs, and they take them to the park to do exercise. Dog can help me with my health.

Finally, he can help us to order my room, or clean my stuff, also he can be my company when I'm doing my homework or eating.
Think, he will wait for you at the night when you come home at evening. You will not eat by yourself. He could be our best friend, and we would have another person in our family. He will make us happy. So, I hope, you see my point.

Teacher Talk

➔ When it comes to creating your word wall, we recommend selecting some of the words from the table on p. 77 rather than posting the table in its entirety. If you write all the words on index cards, you can pick and choose which ones to post at any given time—trade them in and out over the course of the year.

➔ A scaffolding option: Before asking students to incorporate word-wall terms into their own work (Step 5), help them practice choosing appropriate words by having them complete a paragraph in which you've replaced the linking and organizing words with blanks for them to fill in. (Students can fill in the blanks on their own, in pairs, or as a class.) Clarify that there can be more than one correct answer for a given blank (e.g., the words *secondly*, *next*, *after that*, and *then* would all be appropriate choices for introducing the second event in a series).

➔ To give students a sense of the different kinds of linking and organizing words that exist, you can group (or have students group) word-wall terms into categories like the ones on p. 77. Help students recognize that different kinds of writing pieces/purposes call for different kinds of linking and organizing words (e.g., you might expect to find words like *on the other hand* or *on the contrary* in an argument piece that's presenting alternative positions).

➔ Teach students how linking and organizing words can help them understand the relationships between specific sentences, paragraphs, and larger sections of text (a goal of Common Core Reading Standard 5). For example, "The fact that this sentence starts with *on the contrary* tells me it's presenting a different point of view than the preceding sentences."

➔ Explain that linking and organizing words aren't just for writing—that students should use them when speaking as well. Using these kinds of words in their speech will help students express their ideas more clearly and logically (a goal of Common Core Speaking & Listening Standard 4).

➔ Use this tool as an opportunity to teach students that entire *sentences* can have linking and organizing functions (e.g., a sentence that provides a transition between one paragraph and the next). Exploring the function of structural elements like transitional sentences is consistent with the goals of Common Core Reading Standard 5.

Name: Date:

Linking and Organizing Words

To show order or time

First	Second	Next	Then	After that	Finally
Before	At the same time	Subsequently	In the meantime	While	The next step
Earlier	Lastly	First of all	In the first place	To begin with	In conclusion

To introduce facts, reasons, evidence, examples, or additional points

For example	One reason	Another reason	One example	Another example	For instance
First of all	Second of all	Additionally	And	Also	Finally
In addition	Furthermore	Moreover	What's more	As it says here…	As __ notes, "__."

To draw comparisons

Similarly	In the same way	By the same token	Correspondingly	In comparison	Likewise
One similarity	Another similarity	Both	All	As a group	Collectively

To highlight differences or present contrasting ideas/viewpoints

One difference	Another difference	Actually	In fact	On the contrary	In reality
In contrast	However	Although	Instead	But	Yet
Rather	Alternatively	Conversely	On the other hand	Another possibility	Whereas

To conclude, summarize, or discuss causes/effects

To summarize	In conclusion	Finally	As a result	Therefore	Thus
All in all	As expected	On the whole	For these reasons	As shown here	Consequently
Taken together	Because	So	If…then…	Since	In that case

To generalize

In general	On the whole	As a rule	Typically	In most cases	For the most part

To emphasize

Note that	Remember that	Above all	Especially	Importantly	What's more

To clarify

For example	For instance	In other words	To clarify	Specifically	Put another way

RAFT

What is it?

A fun-for-students writing framework (developed by Nancy Vandervanter; see Santa, 1988) that both develops Common Core writing skills and tests students' content knowledge

What are the benefits of using this tool?

The Common Core State Standards remind us that *all* teachers should be working to develop critical writing skills. The problem is that developing meaningful writing tasks across the curriculum can sometimes be challenging. This tool addresses that challenge by presenting a simple framework for developing engaging writing prompts in all content areas. The nature of these prompts trains students to consider task, purpose, personal perspective, and audience (a goal of Writing Standard 4), and the responses that students generate offer valuable insight into their grasp of whatever content they're writing about.

What are the basic steps?

1. Identify something specific you want your students to know or understand (e.g., strategies for staying healthy, reasons Shakespeare is worth reading, the importance of the number zero).
2. Develop a RAFT-specific writing prompt that will test this knowledge/understanding. Your prompt should define the **R**ole students will assume, the **A**udience they'll be addressing, the **F**ormat their writing should take, and their **T**opic or writing task (see pp. 79–80 for ideas and sample prompts).

   Note: Including a strong verb in the task description can help students understand their goal/purpose as writers (e.g., "*Persuade* the school board to…"). Here are some possibilities: *describe*, *argue*, *explain*, *convince*, *create*, *apply*, *analyze*, *summarize*, *invent*, *compare*, *predict*.
3. Share the prompt with students. Discuss the four factors they'll need to consider when writing and how these factors might affect the content/tone/style of what they write.

   ***R**ole:* Who or what are you supposed to be? What is your personal perspective?

   ***A**udience:* For whom are you writing?

   ***F**ormat:* What format will your writing take?

   ***T**opic/task:* What are you writing about? What's your purpose?

   Tip: If students aren't familiar with the format, give them authentic examples to use as models (e.g., real job application letters or newspaper editorials).
4. Use students' completed pieces to assess their understanding of the content and their skills as writers. (Did they write from the appropriate perspective? Tailor their style and message to their audience? Match their language/structure/tone to the given format? Achieve their purpose?)
5. Use what you learn in Step 4 to provide customized feedback and guide future instruction.
6. *Optional:* Have students explain how their task, purpose, and perspective—as determined by their role—affected the content and/or tone of their final pieces (this targets Reading Standard 6).

RAFT: Possible Roles, Audiences, and Formats

Customize the ideas below as needed to fit your content area and goals (e.g., replace *character from a book* with *Holden Caulfield*) or create your own from scratch.

ROLES & AUDIENCES			
Activist	Engineer	Musical instrument	School principal
Advertising agency	Explorer	Newspaper reader	Scientist
Ancient civilization	Family member/Relative	Object of any type	Senior citizen
Animal	Famous artist or musician	Parent	Shape
Audience member	Famous athlete	Part of speech	Someone from the past
Author	Famous document	Passenger/Traveler	Specific atom or molecule
Blogger	Famous road or route	Peers	Speech writer
Body part	Financial planner	Personal hero	Superhero
Business	Food group	Personal trainer	Supreme court justice
Character from a book	Form of government	Picture, image, or graph	Teacher
Coach	Fortune teller	Piece of lab equipment	Textbook publisher
Colleague	Friend	Piece of literature	Therapist
Color	Geological feature	Piece of technology	TV or radio audience
Committee of experts	Grant writer	Place on Earth	TV or radio host
Community leader	Group of students	Plant	Type of equation
Congress	Historical figure	Politician	Type of number
Current event	Immigrant	Process or theory	Vehicle
Disheartened individuals	Inventor	Protestors	Villain (real or fictional)
Doctor	Math problem	Punctuation mark	Voter
Economist	Mechanic	Rebel	World leader
Editor	Military leader or veteran	Reporter	Young children
Enemy	Motivational speaker	School board	Yourself

FORMATS			
Action plan	Email message	Love letter	Research abstract
Analogy	Environmental impact plan	Memoir/Autobiography	Review or critique
Apology letter	Epigraph	Metaphor	Slideshow presentation
Article	Explanatory paragraph	Minutes of a meeting	Slogan
Blog post	Fable	Museum-display placard	Song lyrics
Brochure/Pamphlet	Grant proposal	Myth	Speech
Budget	Illustrated text	Obituary	Text message
Children's book	Instruction manual	Personal narrative	Textbook passage
Classified ad	Interview transcript	Petition	Thank you letter
Comic strip	Invitation	Phone conversation	To-do list
Computer program	Job application	Playbook	Top ten list
Diary or journal entry	Laboratory notebook	Poem	Travelogue
Dictionary entry	Lesson plan	Ransom note	Tweet
Diet or exercise plan	Letter of recommendation	Recipe card	Voicemail message
Editorial	Logical argument	Reminder note	Web page or wiki

How is this tool used in the classroom?

- ✔ To design engaging and educational writing tasks in all content areas
- ✔ To have students write from different perspectives for different purposes and audiences
- ✔ To teach students that point of view and purpose shape the content and style of a text
- ✔ To assess students' understanding of the content they're writing about

Sample prompts are shown below. Note the use of strong-verb task descriptions in the last two.

ROLE: American colonists
AUDIENCE: King George III
FORMAT: Break-up letter
TOPIC: Why we're leaving you

ROLE: Fortune teller
AUDIENCE: *Tyrannosaurus rex*
FORMAT: Warning notice
TOPIC: You're in big trouble! Here's why...

ROLE: Plants
AUDIENCE: Animals
FORMAT: Thank you letter
TOPIC: We appreciate all that you do for us

ROLE: Ancient civilization
AUDIENCE: Future civilization
FORMAT: Advice column
TOPIC: What you can learn from us (good and bad)

ROLE: George from *Of Mice and Men*
AUDIENCE: Self
FORMAT: Diary entry
TOPIC: Why I killed Lennie and how I feel about it

ROLE: Cosine function
AUDIENCE: Therapist
FORMAT: Session transcript
TOPIC: The ups and downs in my life

ROLE: Heart
AUDIENCE: Heart's owner
FORMAT: Action plan
TOPIC: Steps you can take to make my life easier

ROLE: Drifting continent
AUDIENCE: United States Postal Service
FORMAT: Change of address card
TOPIC: Where I'll be in ten million years

ROLE: Cheerleader
AUDIENCE: Vincent van Gogh
FORMAT: Cheer
TOPIC: Why people will love you someday

ROLE: Poem
AUDIENCE: Confused student
FORMAT: Advice column
TOPIC: Here's what I really mean

ROLE: Shakespeare
AUDIENCE: English students who hate him
FORMAT: Top ten list
TOPIC: Why my writing is worth reading

ROLE: First-grade teacher
AUDIENCE: New student
FORMAT: Instruction manual
TOPIC: Classroom rules and procedures

ROLE: Apostrophe
AUDIENCE: Writers everywhere
FORMAT: Plea
TOPIC: Please use me properly!
TASK: *Explain* how writers misuse you, what they can do about it, and why it matters.

ROLE: Scientist
AUDIENCE: Textbook publisher
FORMAT: Petition
TOPIC: Intelligent design
TASK: *Convince* the publisher to include or exclude intelligent design from a future textbook.

EXAMPLE: Elementary social studies

A fourth-grade student's completed RAFT assignment is shown below. Additional responses (same task, different students) can be found at www.ThoughtfulClassroom.com/Tools.

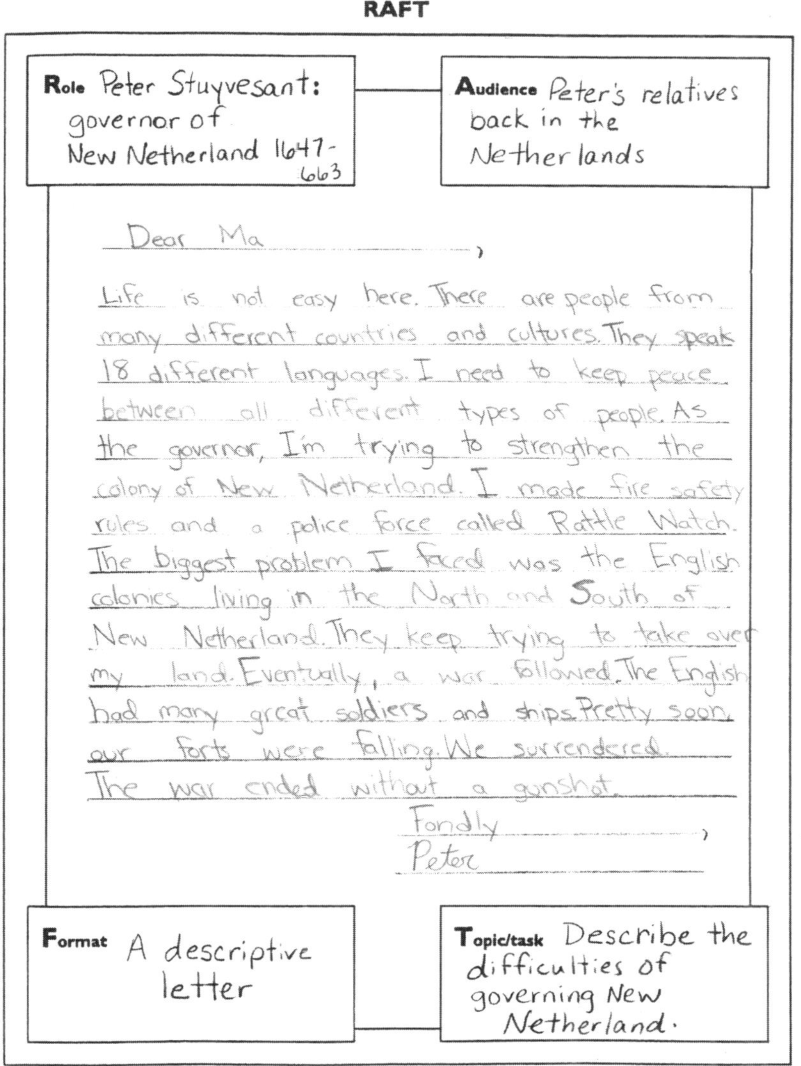
RAFT

Role Peter Stuyvesant: governor of New Netherland 1647-1663

Audience Peter's relatives back in the Netherlands

Dear Ma,

Life is not easy here. There are people from many different countries and cultures. They speak 18 different languages. I need to keep peace between all different types of people. As the governor, I'm trying to strengthen the colony of New Netherland. I made fire safety rules and a police force called Rattle Watch. The biggest problem I faced was the English colonies living in the North and South of New Netherland. They keep trying to take over my land. Eventually, a war followed. The English had many great soldiers and ships. Pretty soon, our forts were falling. We surrendered. The war ended without a gunshot.

Fondly,
Peter

Format A descriptive letter

Topic/task Describe the difficulties of governing New Netherland.

Teacher Talk

→ Teachers often find that the RAFT format appeals to even the most reluctant writers. Some like its clear structure; others like the opportunity to be creative.

→ By giving students the opportunity to write for a wide range of tasks, purposes, and audiences—and by teaching them to adjust their communication style accordingly—RAFT is a great match for Common Core Writing Standards 4 and 10. By helping students appreciate the way that point of view, purpose, and audience shape the content, style, and language of a text or presentation, it supports Reading Standard 6 and Speaking & Listening Standards 4 and 6 as well.

Continued on next page…

➔ If you want students to reap the maximum benefits from this tool, you'll need to teach them what addressing task, purpose, and audience looks like (simply assigning a RAFT task and letting them go won't be good enough). Here are two approaches that can help:

- Work through a RAFT assignment, explaining what you're doing to address task, purpose, and audience. ("Because my task is to present a report to a panel of scientists, I'm going to keep my writing style formal and build in the kinds of content-specific terms a real scientist would use.")
- Help students analyze and learn from completed RAFT assignments (existing samples or ones you create for this purpose) by posing questions like these: What was the writer's role? How did his role affect the content and style of his writing? What type of writing piece is this, and who is the intended audience? Is the structure of the piece, the formality of the language, and the information presented appropriate for this type of writing and this particular audience?

➔ For a change of pace, have students speak (e.g., deliver a speech, podcast, slideshow) or draw their responses instead of writing them. This simple tweak is particularly helpful with very young students. (You could, for example, have students play the **R**ole of a plant, make the **A**udience the sun, make the **F**ormat a picture, and make the **T**opic "how you make me feel.")

➔ Feel free to borrow! RAFT prompts are widely available, both online and in print.

➔ Designing RAFT prompts for specific texts is a fun way to check students' understanding of what they're reading. One option is to record the prompts on the inside covers of books, as suggested by Fisher and Frey (2007). Another option is to have students generate their own prompts for texts that they've read and leave those prompts behind for their classmates to respond to.

➔ Role Definition Charts (the one below is adapted from Buehl, 2009) are a great scaffolding tool. They prepare students for the writing process by helping them think about their roles more deeply.

PERSONALITY	ATTITUDE	INFORMATION	LANGUAGE
Who am I and what are some aspects of my character?	What are my feelings, beliefs, ideas, and/or concerns about this topic?	What do I know that I would want to share with this particular audience?	What kind of language would I use to communicate? Formal? Informal? Literal? Figurative? Any particular tone or dialect?

➔ Train students to look for the RAFT components within writing tasks/test questions (even when those tasks/test questions aren't presented in RAFT format) and craft their responses accordingly. Use sample test items like the one below from the Smarter Balanced Assessment Consortium for practice. Here, students should see that the **R**ole is a writer, the **A**udience is classmates/parents/teacher, the **F**ormat is a magazine article, and the **T**opic/task is to explain what an astronaut's job is like.

> TASK: Your class is creating a magazine about interesting jobs people do. Each person has been assigned to write about a different job. Your assignment is to write an informational article that is several paragraphs long that will help the students in your class know what the job of an astronaut is like. The magazine will be read by the students in your class, parents, and your teacher.

SOURCE: From *Smarter Balanced Assessment Consortium: Practice Test Scoring Guide: Grade 3 Performance Task* by American Institutes for Research, 2013, http://sbac.portal.airast.org/wp-content/uploads/2013/07/Grade3ELAPT.pdf. © 2013 by Smarter Balanced Assessment Consortium.

Name: Date:

RAFT

Role

Audience

Format

Topic/task

Search Party

What is it?

A tool that prepares students to write higher-quality arguments, explanatory pieces, and narratives by reviewing the components these pieces should contain, and by having them search for these components in existing writing samples

What are the benefits of using this tool?

One of the best ways to learn what makes good writing good is to look at examples. Here, students hone their understanding of key Common Core writing components (e.g., claims, reasons, evidence) by locating these components within teacher-provided writing samples. Examining these components in the context of real writing samples helps students see what these components look like and how they're organized. As a result, students are better prepared to incorporate these components into their own writing in a thoughtful and logical way.

What are the basic steps?

1. Determine which Common Core writing type you want to focus on: opinion/argument, informative/explanatory, or narrative. Review the critical components of this writing type as outlined in the Common Core Writing Standards (Standard 1, 2, or 3) for your specific grade level.

Example: A third-grade explanatory piece would include an introduction to the topic, relevant facts/definitions/details, linking words and phrases, and a concluding statement or section.

2. Find or create high-quality, grade-level-appropriate samples of your selected writing type. Be sure that the critical components from Step 1 are clearly evident in these sample pieces.

3. List and discuss the critical components of your selected writing type. Show students what these components look like and model the process of finding them using one or more of the writing samples from Step 2. ("Which sentences in this paragraph introduce the topic? Let's look...")

4. Give students a new writing sample. Break students into "search parties," and ask different parties to search for different components in the given piece. ("Search Party A should find and label the introduction/topic sentence. Search Party B should find and label the linking words...")

5. Have students share their findings with the class and add other groups' findings to their papers. Pose questions that will help them reflect on and apply what they've learned. For example:

What are the key components of an argument? How did this author organize these components within his piece? What kinds of words did he use to link the components together? How might having this information help you the next time you go to write an argument?

6. Use the tool throughout the year with different writing samples and different search assignments.

7. Explain that the ultimate goal of helping students see how other writers have incorporated key components into their pieces is for students to build these same components into their own work. Remind students to do this, and check (have them check as well) that they're actually doing it.

How is this tool used in the classroom?

✔ To develop students' grasp of the key components of Common Core writing types

EXAMPLE 1: Argument (secondary)

Search parties were asked to mark and label the key components of a good argument in the writing sample below. Their combined findings are shown here:

Claim → (Linux is better than other more commonly used operating systems.)(First of all, it's free to obtain unlike other operating systems, which can cost hundreds of dollars to purchase. It also has fewer security issues like viruses, spyware, and adware. A third advantage is that it has a large community of users who are constantly adding and improving programs. This means you don't have to wait until a software company releases a new product to get new programs; you get them constantly!)(Some people say Windows is better because it offers popular programs that Linux doesn't have, but there are comparable programs in Linux that are almost as good.)(Given a choice, people should go with Linux because of the benefits it offers in terms of cost, security, and abundant programs and updates.)

Reasons

Alternate claim + rebuttal

Conclusion

Linking & organizing words are underlined.

EXAMPLE 2: Narrative (primary)

After teaching her students about the elements that compose a good narrative as defined by the Common Core Writing Standards (Standard W.2.3), a second-grade teacher helped them look for those elements as a class using the sample narrative below. Specifically, she and her students looked for *details that described actions, thoughts, and feelings* ("ran into the living room," "my dreams came true," "I was so excited," "jumping up and down and screaming"), *temporal words that indicated the order of events* ("I went," "Next I went," "I couldn't wait anymore, so," "Right then"), and *a conclusion that provided a sense of closure* ("this was the best Christmas ever"). Students then applied what they had learned by working to incorporate these same elements into narratives of their own.

I'll never forget the morning of December 25th. It was still dark outside when I woke up. I went to my parents' room to see if they were awake but they weren't. Next I went to my sister's room, but she was still asleep too. How was that possible? I couldn't wait anymore, so I ran into the living room to see if Santa had come. Right then my dreams came true because the pink bicycle I had been hoping for was right before my eyes. I was so excited I started jumping up and down and screaming. I screamed so loud I woke everyone up, but I didn't care because this was the best Christmas ever!

Teacher Talk

→ The writing samples that you have students analyze can be created by you, by students (e.g., pieces from a previous year's class or from Appendix C of the Common Core ELA/Literacy Standards), or by others (e.g., a textbook passage, research article, or other published piece). Double-spacing the samples will make it easier for students to mark them up.

→ Analyzing existing writing samples to see how individual components function and fit into the overall structure develops Common Core reading skills (Reading Standard 5) as well as writing skills.

Source Savvy

What is it?

A tool that teaches students how to evaluate the quality and usefulness of potential sources

What are the benefits of using this tool?

Assessing the credibility, accuracy, and relevance of potential sources (Common Core Writing Standards 1 and 8, Speaking & Listening Standard 2) has always been an important part of the research process. With the advent of the Internet, which allows just about anyone to publish just about anything, the importance of evaluating potential sources has become even more critical. This tool prepares students to make savvier judgments about the sources they use by providing clear criteria to help them distinguish quality sources from questionable ones.

What are the basic steps?

1. Review the qualities of a good source as defined on the Source Checker (p. 90). Use your judgment (also the requirements of Common Core Writing Standard 8 at your specific grade level) to decide which qualities you want to address.

Example: A fourth-grade teacher might focus on *relevance* (since gathering relevant information is part of the fourth-grade standard) but skip *credibility* (since assessing credibility isn't required until sixth grade).

2. Modify the Source Checker to reflect the qualities you've chosen to focus on. Then introduce and discuss each of these qualities/criteria in detail (see the sample language on p. 87 for ideas). The goal is for students to understand the Source Checker criteria well enough to use them independently.

Note: Letting students discover the qualities of a good source for themselves can help them better understand and internalize these qualities. One way to do this is outlined on p. 89 (upper box).

3. Model the process of using the Source Checker to evaluate a specific source. (Think through the questions aloud, and explain how you use your responses to develop an overall impression.) Evaluate several sources as a class before moving on to Step 4.

Note: The "question boxes" on the Source Checker can be used in different ways. (Students can ponder the questions in their heads and leave the boxes blank; respond with a simple "yes," "sort of," or "no"; or jot down some notes.) The "overall impression" box should be completed as described on the form.

4. Develop/test students' ability to evaluate sources on their own. One way to do this is outlined below. The Source Sort and Select-a-Source variations (p. 88) provide other alternatives.

- Give students a research task and a set of sources to compare (some good, some not so good).
- Ask students to evaluate each source using the criteria on the Source Checker.
- Use students' completed Source Checkers to gauge their ability to evaluate sources effectively.
- Review and remodel the source-checking process for students who still need help.

5. Give students Source Checkers to use when doing independent research. Review their completed Source Checkers so you can evaluate their thinking and offer feedback about their choices.

How is this tool used in the classroom?

✔ To help students assess the quality and usefulness of potential sources

Explaining the criteria on the Source Checker (Step 2) is critical to the success of this tool. The sample language in the box below was designed to give you a sense of what this might sound like in a classroom.

When evaluating the quality of a source, the first thing you might want to check is whether the information is **RELEVANT** to the topic or question you're researching. You might, for example, find a really great book about dinosaurs at the library, but if you're trying to figure out why dinosaurs became extinct, and the book doesn't address that particular topic, would you consider it a good source for this project? No, me neither!

Another aspect of determining whether a source is a useful one involves asking yourself if it's **AGE APPROPRIATE**. If the source is designed for readers who are much younger than you, why might that be problematic? (The information it contains might be too simplistic.) If the source is designed for older, more sophisticated readers, why might that be a problem? (It might be too challenging to make sense of, or contain a level of detail that's beyond what you need.)

Another thing to consider when evaluating a source is whether it's **CURRENT ENOUGH** for your purposes. For some topics, it's critical to use very current sources. (Why, for example, might a two-year-old article about advances in cancer research be problematic?) For other topics, older sources are just fine. (If you wanted to find out what a historical figure like John Calvin was famous for, why might an old encyclopedia entry be "current enough" for your purposes?)

Something else to think about is whether the information in a source is **ACCURATE**. One way to check this is by seeing if you can find the same information in at least one other reputable source. (Some types of sources include reference lists that you can use to check the information they contain; others don't.) Since it's not always possible or practical to check for accuracy directly, you'll want to use credible sources for your research. Why? The information in a credible source is likely to be accurate since credible sources are typically fact-checked before they're published.

So how can you determine whether a source is **CREDIBLE**? A good way to start is to ask yourself whether it was generated by an expert in a relevant field as opposed to a random or potentially unqualified individual. (If you're trying to understand the causes of autism, which would be a more credible source–a group of research scientists or a TV personality? A doctor who specializes in autism or a doctor who specializes in stomach disorders?) Another thing to consider is purpose. Pieces whose purpose is to educate or inform as opposed to sell or persuade are more likely to be objective, and therefore, more likely to be safer sources of accurate information. (Why might an independent reviewer's article about a new computer game be a safer source of accurate information than a press release from the game's developer? Why might a doctor's thoughts on a new fad diet be more objective than the diet's inventor?) Thinking about where you found the information (was it published in a reputable source or by a reputable organization/agency as opposed to a random one?) can also give you some hints about credibility. We'll discuss some sources that are considered reputable in just a bit.

Note: Because *credibility* is the most challenging attribute for students to understand and assess, it's the one that needs the most clarification and discussion. Additional information and suggestions can be found in the Teaching Students About Credibility box on p. 89.

Variation 1: Source Sort

This variation simplifies the source-checking process for students by having them focus on a single criterion. To use it, present students with a hypothetical research question or task and a pile of potential sources. Give them one of the Source Checker criteria to focus on, and have them sort the sources accordingly. (For example, "Sort these into *very relevant*, *somewhat relevant*, and *not relevant* piles," or "Sort these into *seems credible* and *seems questionable* piles.") Have students discuss and defend their choices as a class. ("Which pile did you choose for this source? Why? Does anyone have a different opinion? How come?") Provide feedback and guidance as needed.

Variation 2: Select-a-Source

This variation uses a multiple-choice format to develop and test students' source-checking skills. To use it, present students with a hypothetical research task and a list of possible sources. (The list should include the name of each source as well as a brief description. The sources that you include can be real or made up.) Ask students to pick the best source for the given task and explain their reasoning. Instruct them to refer to the criteria on the Source Checker—or to information they learned while discussing those criteria—when explaining their choices. ("I eliminated Choice A because the information wasn't relevant to the task we were given," or "I eliminated Choice B because it was a sales-oriented site rather than an informational one.") Review and give students feedback about their choices and explanations.

Note: This same type of multiple-choice task can be found on Common Core practice tests developed by the Smarter Balanced Assessment Consortium. A seventh-grade example is shown below.

TASK: A student is preparing to write a research report. Review the student's research plan and the sources that are available. Indicate which source would be *most likely* to contain credible and relevant information.

RESEARCH REPORT PLAN:

Topic: The Colony: The Most Organized of All Animal Social Groups
Audience: Science students
Purpose: To inform
Research question: How do colonies help animals adapt and survive?

POSSIBLE SOURCES:

☐ www.biomebasics.net: Tour the world's biomes without leaving your chair! Explore deserts where termite colonies rise like pillars of sand. Swim oceans where coral reefs teem with life. Survey the vegetation and animal populations of grasslands, forests, and tundra. Can you identify the biomes closest to where you live? Which…

☐ www.krazycolonies.com: Remember those ant farms you had when you were a kid? Well, THEY'RE BACK! Surprise your son or daughter with a colony of creepy-cute ants. From behind a crack-resistant wall of plastic, they'll see drones, soldiers, and that all-important queen, bustling about their buggy business. Only $15.99 and the…

☑ www.animalinfozone.com: Why some animals live in colonies, and how this form of social organization is a key to their survival. In a paper by Dr. Stephen T. Cora, the author shares the work of biologists who have examined the social groups of ants, termites, bees, mole rats, and more…

☐ www.talkingaboutanimals.net: What is an animal colony? Jane Fuller answers questions about insects that live in highly organized social groupings. Her answers may intrigue you, especially her discussion of the term "eusocial"…

SOURCE: Adapted from *Smarter Balanced Assessment Consortium: ELA Practice Test Scoring Guide: Grade 7* by Smarter Balanced Assessment Consortium, 2014, http://sbac.portal.airast.org/wp-content/uploads/2013/08/G7_PracticeTest_ScoringGuide_ELA.pdf. © 2014 by Author.

Helping Students Discover the Qualities of a Good Source

To help students discover the qualities of a good source for themselves, present them with hypothetical research tasks and give them pairs of possible sources for each of the criteria on the Source Checker (one source in the pair should do a good job of satisfying the criterion in question; the other shouldn't). Ask students to compare the sources in each pair, decide which is better for the given task, and explain their reasoning.

Example: To help students discover the importance of a source being current enough, give them a research question that would benefit from current data (e.g., Is Pluto really a planet?) and two possible sources—one that's current enough for the topic (e.g., an article from 2006 or later) and one that isn't (an old encyclopedia entry). Ask students to explain which source would be the better choice for this particular research question and why. ("It looks like Pluto was reclassified after the second source was written, so Source 2 isn't current enough to help us with our question.")

To highlight the idea that current sources aren't always required, you might want to repeat this activity with a research question that doesn't require current information. Here, students should conclude that a new source and an older one might be equally acceptable.

Teaching Students About Credibility

Part of the conversation about credibility should involve teaching students to think about WHO generated the information they're looking at (Is it coming from a reputable organization and/or expert in a relevant field?) and what it means to be an expert (Does the person providing the information have a degree, title, position, or level of experience that qualifies him or her as an expert? Is the person an expert in a *relevant* field?). Clarify that people without special titles or degrees can be just as knowledgeable as documented experts, but that it's typically safer to trust information from someone with known qualifications.

Students should also be taught to think about WHERE their information is coming from (reputable sources vs. questionable ones). Help them understand the types of sources that are considered reputable by discussing general categories of sources that tend to be okay (e.g., material from reputable/objective news sources, US government agencies, museums, peer-reviewed journals, respected professional organizations) as well as specific sources or agencies that are considered reputable (e.g., *National Geographic*, *Scientific American*, *The Wall Street Journal*, *TIME for Kids*, PBS, the CDC). Encourage students to steer clear of websites with unprofessional tones ("People who don't believe in global warming are delusional!!!") or extreme and unsupported positions, as those sites are more likely to have been developed by amateurs than by reputable scholars or agencies.

A third factor for students to consider is purpose (WHY was the source created?). Sources that are trying to persuade or sell something are potentially less credible than sources whose primary goal is to inform or educate. Clarify, however, that the intent to persuade or sell doesn't mean that a source is untrustworthy; it's simply safer to trust a source whose main agenda is to educate.

Finally, use concrete examples to help students learn what credible sources look like. One option is to give students a list of age-appropriate and reputable sources within your discipline. Another is to direct them to a search engine like SweetSearch, which was specifically designed for student use. (The websites it searches have been deemed credible by its staff of research experts, librarians, and teachers.) The regular use of quality sources can help students learn what types of sites, sources, and agencies are considered acceptable.

Name: Date:

Source Checker

SOURCE:

Is the information RELEVANT to your question or task?

Is the information AGE APPROPRIATE?

Is the information CURRENT ENOUGH for your question or task?

Is the information ACCURATE?
Did you find it in a credible source and/or verify it independently?

Is the information CREDIBLE?
WHO generated it? Was it generated by a qualified person, organization, or agency?
WHERE did you find it? Was it published in a reputable source as opposed to a questionable one?
WHY was it presented? Was the primary goal to inform or educate?

OVERALL IMPRESSION:
Explain your reasoning, making sure to refer to the criteria above.

Stop, Read, Revise

What is it?

A process that enhances the quality of student writing by having students read and revise their work

What are the benefits of using this tool?

What students *actually* write isn't always the same as what they think they've written. When they take the time to review their writing, they often find that important words are missing or that their ideas aren't as clear as they thought. Stop, Read, Revise prepares students to root out mistakes and communicate more effectively by training them to review and revise their writing using a specific set of criteria. Collectively, these criteria reinforce a number of Common Core skills, including improving writing via editing and revision (Writing Standard 5); adjusting writing to fit task, purpose, and audience (Writing Standard 4); presenting ideas in a clear and logical way (part of Writing Standards 1–4); and following the conventions of Standard Written English (Language Standards 1 and 2).

What are the basic steps?

1. Talk to students about the importance of reading what they write. Help them generate a list of reasons why the reading-after-writing habit is such a good one to develop.
2. Give students a writing task. Tell them to skip lines so they'll have room to revise their work.
3. Ask students to read their pieces to themselves. Tell them to check their work for The Seven Cs.

   Completeness: Did I leave out any words, details, or big ideas?

   Coherence: Are my ideas presented in a logical and orderly way? Do they make sense?

   Clarity: Are my ideas clear and easy to understand? Is my writing clear and easy to read?

   Correctness: Are there any spelling, grammar, and/or factual errors that I need to correct?

   Composition: Do I have a topic sentence/thesis, supporting information, and conclusion?

   Congruence: Does my response address the specific question, task, or purpose I was given?

   Communication skills: Will my audience "get" what I wrote? Is my tone/language appropriate?

   Tip: Explain the Cs beforehand, and adjust them as needed for specific kinds of writing tasks. With a story, for example, *composition* might become "Do I have a clear beginning, middle, and end?"
4. Instruct students to revise their work as needed.
5. Invite students to reflect on and share what they learned by reading their own writing.
6. Teach students that the Stop, Read, Revise process is one that they can and should use on their own. Help them make it habitual by having them use it as often as possible.

How is this tool used in the classroom?

✔ To help students evaluate and improve the quality of their written work

Writing Frames

What is it?

A collection of customizable writing frames that can be used to assess students' content knowledge, develop specific writing skills, and promote regular writing

What are the benefits of using this tool?

With the Common Core State Standards' emphasis on writing, it's more important than ever to get students writing on a regular basis. This tool makes that easier to do by presenting a collection of writing frames and prompts to choose from. Besides engaging students in a range of writing tasks, as called for by Writing Standard 10, these frames and prompts can be used to

- assess students' understanding of key content/texts at any point in a learning sequence;
- give students practice crafting the kinds of writing pieces that standardized tests require; and
- develop and test a variety of thinking/writing skills, many of which have ties to the Common Core.

What are the basic steps?

1. Identify the content knowledge/skills that you want to develop or assess. Do you want to test students' understanding of supply and demand? Their ability to summarize the key points from a text? Their ability to identify discrepancies between one author's presentation of events and another's?
2. Review the writing frames on p. 93 (there are thirteen CREATIVE IDEAS to choose from). Decide which of the frames best meets your needs. Pick one of the corresponding writing prompts and customize it to fit your content and goals—or develop a prompt from scratch.
3. Present the writing prompt to students and help them determine what it's asking them to do. For example, are they being asked to make a comparison? Summarize data? Argue a position?
4. Tell students how and when to respond. Should they tackle the writing prompt with a partner? On their own? During class? For homework? Is there a time limit? Do they need to polish their writing?
5. Discuss the criteria for success. Make it clear that a high-quality response should demonstrate students' knowledge of the content *and* their command of the relevant thinking/writing skills.
6. Review students' responses to determine whether there are any aspects of the content or any thinking/writing skills that you should review or reteach.

FRAMES	WRITING PROMPTS ASK STUDENTS TO...
Compare & contrast	*Compare and/or contrast two or more items or texts. For example:* • Compare and contrast these ___ (items, individuals, processes, approaches, solutions, texts, versions). • Are ___ and ___ more similar or different? Support your answer using specific details/examples. • Which of these items are most similar? Which are most different? Explain your reasoning.
Relate personally	*Make a personal (or real-world) connection to the content. For example:* • How would you feel/what would you do if you were ___ (e.g., a historical figure or literary character)? • How is this relevant to your life? • How can you apply what you learned?
Evaluate	*Assess or judge something using specific criteria. For example:* • Which idea/strategy/solution/product/model is best? Why? What criteria did you use to decide? • Did this person/character make the right decision? Why? • Evaluate the soundness of this author's/individual's ___ (claim, evidence, approach, conclusion, solution).
Associate	*Generate associations or explain how given items/ideas are connected. For example:* • What comes to mind when I say ___? What comes to mind when you see/hear/taste/touch/smell ___? • How is ___ like a ___? • How are these two ___ (concepts, characters, objects, ideas, individuals) connected?
Trace/ sequence	*Describe the course, development, or sequence of something. For example:* • Trace the development/evolution of this ___ (event, character, idea, invention, story line, theme). • Trace the argument and specific claims in this text. • Trace the sequence of steps that you used to ___ (or that are involved in ___).
Interpret/ analyze	*Interpret/analyze data, decisions, text passages, etc. For example:* • What can you conclude from this data? Why? • What is the meaning of this passage/parable/image/law/quotation/dream? Why do you think so? • Analyze how or why ___. (Example: How an author structured a text or why an experiment failed)
Validate	*Validate (or evaluate the validity of) a conclusion, statement, source, etc. For example:* • Is this a valid ___ (argument, solution, conclusion, criticism, model)? Why or why not? • How did you check the validity/reliability of ___? (Example: Validity of a model or reliability of a source) • How do you know that ___ is the case? Describe your evidence.
Explain	*Explain what, why, or how. For example:* • What do you know about ___? Write an explanatory paragraph. • Explain why ___. • Explain how ___.
Identify & describe	*Describe an observation, object, relationship, individual, event, etc. For example:* • Identify and describe something you observed (property, pattern, discrepancy, etc.). • Describe the relationship between ___ and ___. • Describe who/how/what happened ___. (Example: Describe what Ping chooses to do and why.)
Define	*Define a critical term, concept, or problem. For example:* • Define the following concept or term in your own words: ___. • What makes a ___ a ___? What are its critical characteristics? (Example: What makes a sonnet a sonnet?) • Define a problem that ___ (or one that can be solved/addressed by ___).
Explore possibilites	*Explore alternatives, possibilities, and "what if" scenarios. For example:* • What is another way of ___? What is another explanation for ___? How many possible ___ can you ___? • What if ___? What might be the consequences if ___? (Example: What if the decimal point didn't exist?) • Why or how might ___? (Example: How might we improve the cost-effectiveness of this design?)
Argue a position	*Support a position/claim (theirs or someone else's) with solid reasons and evidence. For example:* • State your position on ___ (or construct an argument that ___) and support it with evidence. • Do you agree or disagree with ___? Explain your answer using specific evidence, examples, or details. • Provide evidence to support or refute the claim that ___.
Summarize	*Summarize what they read, observed, heard, or experienced. For example:* • To summarize, what I read/heard/learned was ___. • The most important point or takeaway message was ___. • Summarize this information in a visual format (e.g., sketch, chart, data table).

SOURCE: Adapted from *Tools for Thoughtful Assessment* (p. 175), by A. L. Boutz, H. F. Silver, J. W. Jackson, and M. J. Perini, 2012, Ho-Ho-Kus, NJ: Thoughtful Education Press. © 2012 by Silver Strong & Associates. Adapted with permission.

How is this tool used in the classroom?

✔ To get students writing on a regular basis

✔ To assess students' grasp of key content and texts

✔ To develop the thinking and writing skills that today's standards demand

The writing frames on p. 93 (italicized in the list below) can be used for a variety of purposes:

- They can be used to engage students in writing routinely for a wide range of tasks and purposes (Common Core W.CCR.10). To do this, simply choose different frames throughout the year.
- They can be used to test students' understanding of key content. A chemistry teacher, for example, might see if students can *explain* how to balance a chemical equation. (Note that writing tasks can be assigned at the start, middle, or end of a unit—and for formative or summative purposes.)
- They can be used to give students practice writing the kinds of pieces that standardized tests require—for example, comparisons, arguments, explanations, and summaries.
- They can be used to develop the kinds of thinking skills that the Common Core State Standards and Next Generation Science Standards demand—for example, comparing, validating, evaluating, explaining, arguing, summarizing, and interpreting.
- They can be used to generate writing prompts that target specific standards. Here are some examples:
  - — *Define* the role an illustrator plays in telling a story. (Common Core RL.K.6)
  - — *Interpret* this graph. *Explain* how it helps us grasp the author's point. (Common Core RI.4.7)
  - — *Compare* these two accounts of Columbus's discovery of America. *Identify & describe* any discrepancies. (Common Core RI.8.9)
  - — *Explain* how the author's point of view is conveyed in this article. (Common Core RI.6.6)
  - — *Evaluate* the degree to which the author's proposed solution is supported by solid evidence. (Common Core RST.9–10.8)
  - — *Identify & describe* a pattern we noticed when comparing early morning temperatures to late afternoon temperatures. (Next Generation Science Standard K-ESS2-1)
  - — *Explore possibilities:* Describe the different two-dimensional cross sections that can be generated by slicing a right rectangular prism in different ways. (Common Core 7.G.A.3)

Teacher Talk

➔ Prepare students to be successful by teaching/modeling the thinking and writing skills that different frames and prompts require. ("To write an argument piece, we'd start by...") Continue the teaching and modeling process until students are capable of crafting quality responses on their own.

➔ For variety (or when using the tool with very young students), you can have students discuss the prompts as a class instead of responding to them in writing. While this approach doesn't develop writing skills, it does still develop the thinking skills that are embedded in the prompts themselves.

Speaking & Listening Tools

It was impossible to get a conversation going. Everybody was talking too much.

—Yogi Berra

Talking matters for learning. Although it's possible to think without talking—and to talk without much thinking—each can strengthen the other. Talking also provides windows into what students are learning. I want schools to be places of rich learning, and therefore I want them to be places of rich talk.

—Elizabeth A. City, "Talking to Learn"

If we expect students to be prepared for college-level work and the demands of today's workplaces, then they need "ample opportunities to take part in rich, structured conversations...built around important content" (NGA Center/CCSSO, 2010, p. 48). But these kinds of conversations don't just happen organically. To make them a reality in the classroom, we must help our students become engaged and active participants who are able to listen attentively and respectfully, evaluate and summarize other people's ideas, and express and support their own.

Preparing students for college and career success also entails teaching them to develop clear and organized presentations that are consistent with task, purpose, and audience—and that contain thoughtfully selected visuals. This chapter features five tools that can help students both develop these critical presentations skills and become more productive members of classroom conversations.

These are the five tools:

1. **Participation Techniques** encourages active and productive participation in classroom conversations by teaching students simple moves for getting involved.
2. **Pictures with a Purpose** teaches students to use images and other media thoughtfully, and for the purpose of enhancing the quality of their work.
3. **Presentation Planner** uses a ten-question planning template to guide and improve students' work on classroom presentations.

4. **Speak-Up Stems** encourages students to speak up during classroom conversations by giving them specific suggestions (in the form of sentence stems) about what they might say.

5. **What I Hear You Saying Is...** promotes active listening by requiring students to restate what others have said in their own words.

Note: Because this chapter only contains five tools, it's worth mentioning that tools from other chapters also target Common Core speaking and listening skills. Here are some examples:

- **Knee-to-Knee Conference** (p. 65) and **Gallery Walk** (pp. 57–61) encourage the kinds of collaborative, small-group conversations called for by Common Core Speaking & Listening Standard 1.
- **Gallery Walk** (pp. 57–61) develops students' capacity to identify and integrate key ideas from different types of sources (Speaking & Listening Standard 2).
- **Claim Check** (pp. 17–18) and **Choose Your Evidence** (pp. 14–16) train students to evaluate claims and identify quality evidence—skills that are central to Speaking & Listening Standard 3.

Participation Techniques

What is it?

A tool that encourages active and productive participation in classroom conversations

What are the benefits of using this tool?

In many classrooms, the teacher's voice is heard far more often than that of the students. This tool promotes a higher level of student talk by teaching students simple techniques for engaging in classroom conversations. Collectively these techniques help students exhibit the productive conversation behaviors that the Common Core State Standards call for—behaviors like responding to and developing what others have said, asking questions, and evaluating ideas (see Speaking & Listening Standards 1 and 3).

What are the basic steps?

1. Share the goal of this tool (to encourage more student talk during classroom conversations) and its value (students who actively participate learn more than those who don't).
2. Prepare a list of simple but specific things that students can do to participate productively in classroom conversations. Here are some possibilities:
   - Ask a relevant question (questions can be directed toward the teacher or a classmate).
   - Agree or disagree with someone/something and explain why.
   - Make a comparison or draw a connection (to everyday life, to another topic, to a text, etc.).
   - Expand on an idea or apply it to another context.
   - String together/summarize/synthesize what's been said.
   - Take and/or support a position.
   - Offer relevant facts, details, or examples.
   - Share and discuss alternatives (solutions, viewpoints, applications, etc.).
   - Analyze or evaluate something (decision, solution, aspect of a text, use of logic/evidence, etc.).
3. Post the list of participation techniques in an easily visible location so students can refer to it throughout the year. Model the techniques for students so they're clear about how to use them.
4. Clarify that the techniques should be used during small-group, student-student conversations as well as during whole-class, teacher-led discussions.
5. Prompt students to use the techniques on a regular basis. ("We haven't heard from you today, Billy. Can you use one of our participation techniques to respond to what Jae just said?")

How is this tool used in the classroom?

✔ To promote active participation and engagement during classroom conversations

✔ To develop critical speaking and listening skills

Variation 1: Wheel of Participation

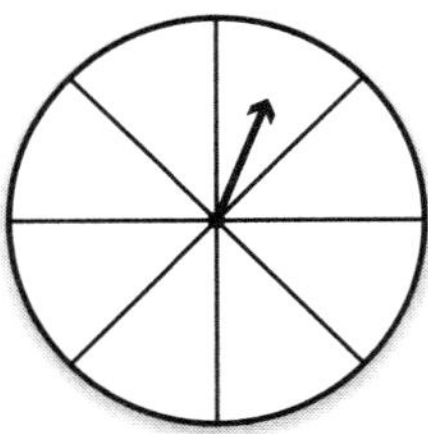

For a fun twist, create a spinner wheel like the one shown here (include some or all of the participation techniques on the wheel). When you call on a student during a classroom lesson or discussion, spin the spinner, and have that student respond using whichever technique the spinner lands on. If the technique doesn't fit the context of the conversation you're having, allow the student to spin again.

Variation 2: Playing Your Participation Cards

To encourage students to participate in different ways, create decks of "participation cards" (sets of index cards with one participation technique listed on each card). Give one deck to each student and encourage students to "play all their cards" over the course of a week. ("Once you use a particular technique, you can take that card out of your deck. The goal is to use up your entire deck by the end of the week.") If you want, you can invite students to personalize and spiff up their decks by drawing icons for the individual techniques on the backs of their cards.

Teacher Talk

→ Primary-grade teachers (or any teachers for that matter) may want to use icons rather than words when creating their lists of participation techniques. Try a question mark for "ask a relevant question," a thumbs up/thumbs down symbol for "agree or disagree with something/someone," etc.

→ If you're having trouble getting students to participate, try distributing the list of Speak-Up Stems on p. 107. This list encourages participation by highlighting specific language that students can use to get involved in classroom conversations.

→ The ultimate goal is for students to use the participation techniques independently, without you reminding them. Help students develop this habit, both by prompting them to use the techniques on a regular basis (Step 5), and by noting when the techniques are used ("Luke just used one of the techniques on our list to keep the conversation going. Who can tell me which one he used?").

Pictures with a Purpose

What is it?

A tool that prepares students to use visuals and other media as a means of enhancing their spoken and written presentations

What are the benefits of using this tool?

Look at a primary-grade student's illustrated story and you'll likely see illustrations that make sense (typically, pictures of whatever characters, events, or items that student is writing about). Sit through a typical high school student's slideshow, on the other hand, and you're more likely to encounter random images and sound clips than relevant ones. This tool trains students of all ages to be more thoughtful about the "extras" they add to their written pieces and presentations. In doing so, it supports the Common Core's call for students to use visuals and other media in a purposeful rather than decorative way (Speaking & Listening Standard 5, Writing Standard 2).

What are the basic steps?

1. Discuss the idea that "extras" (e.g., drawings, photos, or sound clips) should serve to enhance students' work in some way—in other words, that every addition should have a clear purpose.
2. Discuss possible purposes/reasons for adding these kinds of extras (see the handout on p. 102 for ideas). Use concrete examples to illustrate the various purposes. ("How does the picture on this page create mood or atmosphere?")
3. Give students something to illustrate (e.g., a text passage, slide, or scientific process/procedure). Provide images for them to choose from, or have them create or search for images on their own.
4. Encourage students to be thoughtful about their choices and additions. ("Hmmm...Which of these elephant images will best achieve my purpose? Since my goal is to illustrate the physical features of an Asian elephant specifically, this cartoon of a generic elephant isn't going to work!")
5. Have students indicate the general purpose of each addition by checking the appropriate box(es) on the handout. Then ask them to explain each addition a bit more specifically. For example:

> General purpose = ☑ To show something that is being described
> Specifically, I added this sketch in order to help people see where a dorsal fin is located.

> General purpose = ☑ To emphasize an important point and ☑ help people visualize a location
> Specifically, I added this map in order to show how far Christianity spread between 300–600 AD.

6. Clarify that the ultimate goal is for students to enhance their own written pieces and presentations with thoughtfully selected extras. Remind them that every addition should have a clear purpose.

How is this tool used in the classroom?

✔ To encourage the strategic incorporation of images, sound clips, videos, etc.

EXAMPLE 1: Primary science

Second graders were asked to illustrate key terms/concepts from an informational text about the life cycle of a chicken. One student's illustration is shown below, as is the explanation he gave for adding it. (Notice how this teacher simplified the reproducible handout by deleting the checklist and having students explain their additions in their own words.)

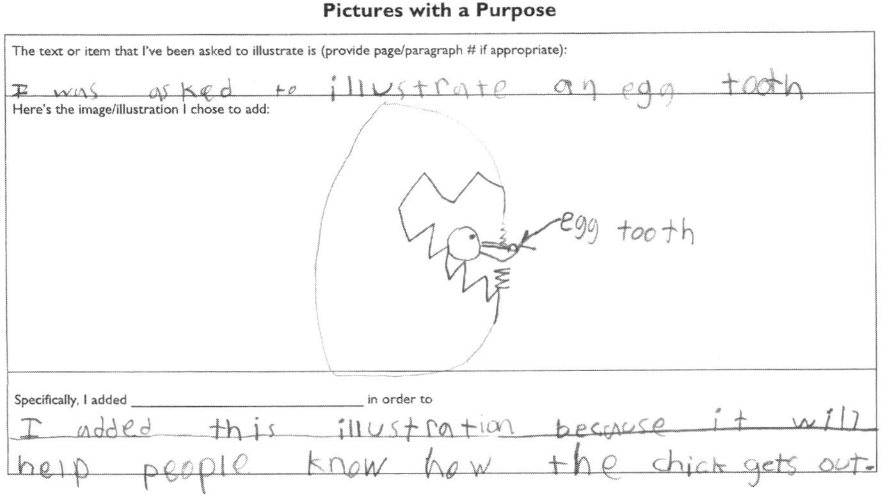
Pictures with a Purpose

The text or item that I've been asked to illustrate is (provide page/paragraph # if appropriate):

I was asked to illustrate an egg tooth

Here's the image/illustration I chose to add:

Specifically, I added ______ in order to

I added this illustration because it will help people know how the chick gets out.

EXAMPLE 2: Elementary ELA

Third graders were asked to add a purposeful illustration to Chapter 17 from *Charlotte's Web* (White, 1952) and then explain their purpose for adding it. The illustration that one student generated to highlight and help people visualize the setting is shown below.

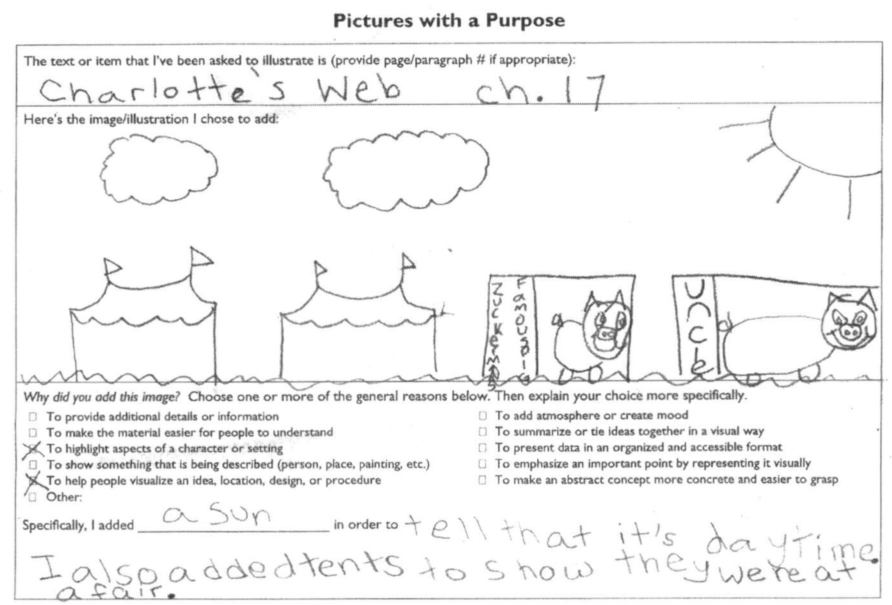
Pictures with a Purpose

The text or item that I've been asked to illustrate is (provide page/paragraph # if appropriate):

Charlotte's Web ch. 17

Here's the image/illustration I chose to add:

Why did you add this image? Choose one or more of the general reasons below. Then explain your choice more specifically.

- ☐ To provide additional details or information
- ☐ To make the material easier for people to understand
- ☒ To highlight aspects of a character or setting
- ☐ To show something that is being described (person, place, painting, etc.)
- ☒ To help people visualize an idea, location, design, or procedure
- ☐ Other:
- ☐ To add atmosphere or create mood
- ☐ To summarize or tie ideas together in a visual way
- ☐ To present data in an organized and accessible format
- ☐ To emphasize an important point by representing it visually
- ☐ To make an abstract concept more concrete and easier to grasp

Specifically, I added a sun in order to tell that it's daytime. I also added tents to show they were at a fair.

EXAMPLE 3: Secondary science

AP Biology students were given a PowerPoint slide with nothing but a title on it and asked to add images that the person presenting the slide could use to illustrate and explain the concept described in the title. One student's completed slide is shown at the right.

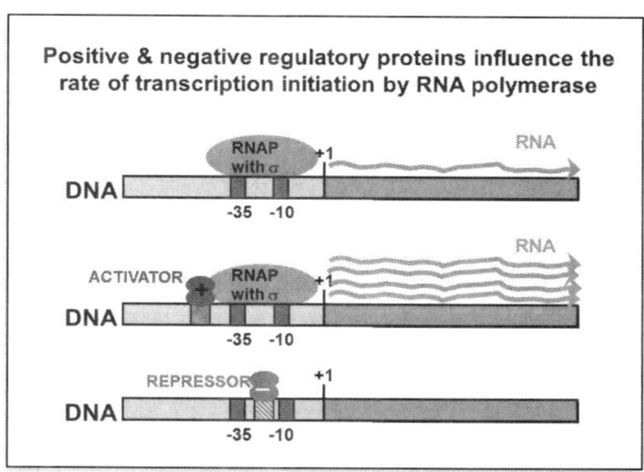

Teacher Talk

- ➔ When starting out (or when using the tool with younger students), you can simplify things by asking students to add an illustration/other addition for a specific purpose rather than having them select a purpose themselves. You might, for example, ask them to "add a picture that *shows how the main character is feeling* at this point in the story" or "create a graphic that *summarizes the results of our class poll* in a visual way." Other scaffolding options include shortening and/or simplifying the "Why did I add this image?" checklist that appears on the handout (p. 102) or forgoing the handout entirely and reviewing the checklist options verbally.
- ➔ Clarify that a single addition can serve multiple purposes. (A student might, for example, add a picture both to aid comprehension and to depict something that's being described in the text.) If adding a multipurpose extra, students should check off all appropriate boxes on the checklist.
- ➔ Encourage students to include specific details, words, or phrases from whatever texts they're illustrating when explaining their additions (Step 5). For example, "I drew this picture to show how sad Gloria felt when Frances told her she was too little to play ball."
- ➔ Invite students to compare their additions with those of their classmates. Facilitate a discussion about which are the best and why. ("Jon's image does the best job of setting the mood because…")
- ➔ Once students are comfortable adding sketches and images, you can have them branch out to other types of media. Since the handout was designed for adding sketches/images specifically, students using other types of media would complete the top and bottom boxes only.
- ➔ Encourage students to consult the "Why did I add this image?" checklist whenever they're adding extras to a written piece or presentation to ensure that each addition has a valid purpose. You can facilitate this behavior by having students keep a copy of the checklist in their notebooks.

Variation: What's the Picture's Purpose?

For a change of pace, challenge students to explain and evaluate the impact of images that others have added instead of adding images themselves. ("How does the figure from this textbook passage add to or reflect the text that it's part of? Why might the textbook's developer have added it?") Asking students to do this kind of analysis targets elements of Common Core Reading Standard 7.

Name: Date:

Pictures with a Purpose

The text, section of text, or item that I've been asked to illustrate is:

Here's the image/illustration I chose to add:

Why did I add this image? (Choose one or more of the general reasons below. Then explain your choice more specifically.)

- ☐ To provide additional details or information
- ☐ To make the material easier for people to understand
- ☐ To highlight aspects of a character or setting
- ☐ To show something that is being described (person, place, painting, etc.)
- ☐ To help people visualize an idea, location, design, or procedure
- ☐ Other:
- ☐ To add atmosphere or create mood
- ☐ To summarize or tie ideas together in a visual way
- ☐ To present data in an organized and accessible format
- ☐ To emphasize an important point by representing it visually
- ☐ To make an abstract concept more concrete and easier to grasp

Specifically, I added ______________________ in order to:

Presentation Planner

What is it?

A tool that uses ten simple guiding questions to structure students' work on classroom presentations

What are the benefits of using this tool?

For many students, presentations are all about the bells and whistles. Instead of clear, well-organized presentations that reflect task, purpose, and audience, students give us fancy slide transitions, decorative backgrounds, and things popping on and off the screen. This tool uses a simple, ten-question planning template to refocus students' attention on what's important. The questions on the template address the fundamentals of a high-quality presentation as defined both by the Common Core Speaking & Listening Standards (Standards 4–6) and by our own experience.

What are the basic steps?

1. Talk to students about the importance of planning out a presentation before designing it. Show them how the questions on the Presentation Planner (pp. 104–105) can help them do this.

   Tip: Adjust the questions on the planner as needed to target whatever presentation skills the Common Core Speaking & Listening Standards emphasize at your particular grade level.

2. Present an assignment that requires students to give a presentation (e.g., a slideshow or poster).
3. Instruct students to complete their planners *before* working on their presentation materials. (They can use extra pages if space becomes an issue.) Prepare them for success by doing the following:
   - Discuss strategies for responding to the questions on the planner. For example, "If I know that audience members will be unfamiliar with my topic, I might provide extra background information or connect my material to things they're familiar with."
   - Clarify the difference between using visuals/multimedia components for the sake of using them and using them strategically as called for by Common Core Speaking & Listening Standard 5. The Pictures with a Purpose tool (pp. 99–102) can help.
4. Give students feedback about their completed planners.
5. Remind students to consult their planners as they work on their presentations.
6. Give students feedback about their completed presentations. Be sure to address items from the planner—for example, the degree to which the presentation achieved its purpose or was tailored to its audience.
7. Encourage students to use Presentation Planners whenever they're preparing a presentation—not just when you tell them to. Make blank planners available for this purpose.

How is this tool used in the classroom?

✔ To help students improve the quality of classroom presentations via advance planning

Name: Date:

Presentation Planner, page 1

1. What is the TOPIC of my presentation?

2. What is the goal or PURPOSE of my presentation?

3. What INFORMATION is critical for me to present? (List the big ideas and key details/examples.)

4. What FORMAT will I use to deliver my information? (Slideshow? Poster? Podcast? Something else?)

5. Where might I find relevant information? What SOURCES will I consult? (books, Internet, maps, teacher, etc.)

Name: Date:

Presentation Planner, page 2

6. Who is my AUDIENCE? What background knowledge, interests, and/or needs might my audience have?

7. How will I ADAPT my content, language, and presentation style to fit my audience and my purpose?

8. How might I use VISUALS or other media to enhance my audience's understanding of the material?

9. How will I try to ENGAGE my audience? CONFIRM that audience members are understanding and following me?

10. How can I ORGANIZE my information so that it's easy to follow?
Consider a few different possibilities. Then OUTLINE or sketch out your plan on a separate page.

Speak-Up Stems

What is it?

A tool that encourages students to speak up during classroom conversations by providing them with a list of options for what they might say (e.g., "I agree with your position because___," "That seems similar to ___," or "Have you considered the possibility that ___?")

What are the benefits of using this tool?

The Common Core Speaking & Listening Standards stress the importance of involving students in a variety of rich and structured conversations. In order for students to reap the benefits of these conversations, however, they must be active and engaged participants—participants who express and defend their positions, ask and answer questions, develop what others have said, and evaluate/synthesize ideas (Standards 1 and 3). This tool prepares students to fulfill these and other productive conversation criteria by teaching them simple moves for speaking up in class. These moves come in the form of sentence stems that highlight language students can use to get involved in classroom conversations.

What are the basic steps?

1. Share the goal of this tool (to encourage students to participate productively during classroom conversations) and its value (active participation facilitates learning).
2. Distribute and review the list of Speak-Up Stems on p. 107. Shorten and/or modify the list as needed.
3. Prompt students to use these stems during whole-class or small-group discussions. ("We haven't heard from you yet, Tamia. Can you add something to the conversation? Use the list of stems if you need help.")
4. Clarify that the stems are only there to help students, and that they can use their own words if they prefer.

How is this tool used in the classroom?

✔ To promote active participation and engagement during classroom conversations
✔ To develop critical speaking and listening skills

Teacher Talk

➔ This tool is similar to the Participation Techniques tool (pp. 97–98) in that both are designed to encourage productive contributions to classroom conversations. The difference is that Participation Techniques presents general strategies for participating (e.g., ask a question or state a position), whereas this tool provides specific suggestions about what to say (a more scaffolded approach). Ideally, the tools should be used together so that students are exposed to both general strategies and specific options for implementing them.

Name: Date:

Speak-Up Stems

I agree/disagree because ________________.

I believe ________________ because ________________.

I've changed my opinion on this because ________________.

That reminds me of/seems similar to ________________.

What I think I heard you saying was ________________.

Can you explain how you arrived at that position/solution/conclusion?

What assumptions, values, or beliefs is your position based on?

Have you considered ________________ (an alternative viewpoint, solution, angle, or data set)?

I'm not sure I follow you. Can you clarify your reasoning for me? Or give me an example?

Can someone help me understand ________________?

To expand on what ________________ (name of person) said, ________________.

An example of that might be ________________.

It seems like the most important point here is ________________.

So, to summarize so far, ________________.

If we put these ideas together, ________________.

What I Hear You Saying Is...

What is it?

A paraphrasing tool that challenges students to restate what others have said in their own words

What are the benefits of using this tool?

Looking for a simple, no-prep-required technique that produces a wide variety of learning benefits? Look no further! As teachers, we can achieve a number of benefits simply by asking our students to paraphrase what they've heard (or read). Among other things, making this simple move

- forces students to focus and pay attention, because they'll have to paraphrase what they've heard;
- promotes understanding and retention by having students restate key points in their own words;
- helps us and our students identify and address gaps in understanding or attention; and
- develops Common Core speaking and listening skills (listening with care, reviewing key ideas).

What are the basic steps?

1. Begin a lecture, presentation, or classroom discussion. Stop periodically and call on students to paraphrase what they've just heard you, a classmate, or someone else say.

2. If students give inaccurate or incomplete responses, review (or have a student review) the material in question and let them try again, or use probing questions to help them. For example:

   Teacher: What was the main thing the narrator was trying to tell us in this segment of the video?

   Student: I heard the narrator say we need to look at our clients before starting to cut their hair.

   Teacher: That's true. Do you recall what he said about *why* we should do that?

   Student: Oh yeah, he said it's because different haircuts look better on difference face shapes.

3. Explain that students can benefit from using this technique on their own. Encourage them to review key details in their heads or on paper when listening to lectures, reading assigned texts, etc.

How is this tool used in the classroom?

✔ To promote attention and active listening

✔ To help students understand and remember what they've heard (or read)

✔ To identify and correct gaps in understanding

Teacher Talk

➔ Having students paraphrase on paper *before* calling on anyone forces all students to pay attention and construct their own understanding of what they've heard. Another way to get everyone paying attention is to call on a variety of students, not just those who raise their hands.

➔ Encourage students to use this format when paraphrasing: "What I heard ___ (name of speaker) say is ___." Invite the original speaker to make corrections as needed. ("Actually, I was saying ___.")

Language Tools

"When I use a word," Humpty Dumpty said, in rather a scornful tone, "it means just what I choose it to mean—neither more nor less."

—Lewis Carroll, *Through the Looking-Glass*

As teachers, we constantly strive to create a classroom environment where children are exposed to high quality language in varying forms. After all, language acquisition and its use are at the core of all the reading, writing, and communication we expect of our students.

—Genia Connell, "12 Steps to Creating a Language-Rich Environment"

One might be tempted to claim that the Common Core's inclusion of a separate strand of standards for language is redundant since the other standards—reading, writing, and speaking and listening—are all about the processes that students use to understand language and communicate well. But one of the clearest cases for giving language its own set of standards has to do with vocabulary acquisition. Since disparities in academic achievement have been traced to differences in vocabulary knowledge (NGA Center/CCSSO, 2010, Appendix A), enhancing students' vocabularies needs to be a top priority in today's classrooms.

This chapter's six vocabulary-building tools help students acquire the diverse word knowledge that college and career readiness demands by targeting a wide range of terms—everything from terms that can enhance students' writing and test-taking abilities to terms that can help students communicate like experts in various disciplines. Unlike many traditional vocabulary tools, the focus isn't on having students memorize dictionary definitions, but rather on helping students understand words deeply, recognize word relationships, use new words when speaking and writing, and decipher word meanings independently.

The seventh and final tool in this chapter is a flexible one that can be used to develop and test a variety of critical language skills, including the ability to follow the conventions of Standard Written English.

These are the seven tools:

1. **3C Word Walls** transforms classroom word walls from passive displays to interactive learning tools that promote three important "Cs": **C**omprehension of critical content, improved **C**ommunication skills, and **C**ommon Core success.

2. **Concept Definition Map** deepens students' understanding of critical terms and concepts by helping students develop deep, detailed, and personally meaningful definitions.

3. **Task & Test Verbs** facilitates test success by familiarizing students with the meanings of verbs that commonly appear in task-and-test prompts—verbs like *analyze*, *evaluate*, *compare*, and *support*.

4. **Vocabulary Storytellers** tests students' ability to use new words in context by inviting students to build those words into original stories.

5. **Word Arrays** helps students understand subtle differences in word meanings by having them explore the definitions of related words and order those words along a continuum; students then reflect on the impact of using one word over another.

6. **Word Detectives** prepares students to become more independent vocabulary learners and readers by teaching them how to use context clues to develop working definitions of unfamiliar terms.

7. **You Be the Teacher** develops and tests students' understanding of targeted language skills by challenging students to find and correct the errors in teacher-provided work samples.

3C Word Walls

What is it?

A tool that shows how word walls can be used to promote three important "Cs": **C**omprehension, **C**ommunication skills (oral and written), and **C**ommon Core success

What are the benefits of using this tool?

Word walls are a mainstay of elementary classrooms, where they're used to highlight high-frequency sight words and word families. Here, we describe four alternative types of word walls that are just as appropriate for high school classrooms as they are for elementary ones: domain-specific word walls, transitional word walls, descriptive word walls, and "task & test verb" word walls. Collectively, these four different kinds of walls prepare students to comprehend critical content, communicate more effectively, and respond appropriately to Common Core-based test questions.

What are the basic steps?

1. Familiarize yourself with the different types of word walls described on pp. 112–115. Decide which type you'll create and the words you'll include.
2. Record your words on index cards or strips of paper (words should be large enough for students to see from their seats). Ensure that students will be able to rearrange and interact with the words by hanging them on an easily accessible board using tacks, magnets, or Velcro.
3. Introduce the word wall. (What type is it? What kind of words are on it? What is its purpose?)
4. Teach or review the meanings of the words using any strategies you want. (This can be done all at once or over the course of a unit.) Post a student-friendly definition for each term.

   Tip: Invite students to personalize and take ownership of the wall by adding images, drawings, synonyms/antonyms, examples, and/or objects that help them grasp the meanings of the words.
5. Use word-wall terms as often as possible when speaking and writing (point to the wall or underline the words to help students make the connection). Encourage students to do the same.
6. Make word-wall activities part of your regular classroom routine. Ideas for getting students to engage with, use, and demonstrate their knowledge of word-wall terms can be found on pp. 112–115.
7. Facilitate continued use of word-wall terms by making them accessible throughout the year. When a new wall goes up, store old words in a recipe-card box, on a key ring, etc.

How is this tool used in the classroom?

✔ To help students develop a rich and varied vocabulary of domain-specific and general terms
✔ To promote comprehension, communication skills, and Common Core success
✔ To transform classroom word walls from passive displays to interactive learning tools

Domain-Specific Word Walls

Description/Purpose:

Domain-specific word walls develop students' understanding of discipline-specific terms and concepts from particular units of study.

How these word walls develop the 3Cs:

These walls support the **C**ommon Core State Standards' call for students to acquire a range of discipline-specific vocabulary terms (L.CCR.6). As such, they prepare students both to **C**omprehend critical course material and **C**ommunicate more precisely, using the language of experts in the field (W.CCR.2, L.CCR.3).

Creating your wall:

Select discipline-specific terms that relate to one or more units of study (e.g., the bold-faced words from a textbook chapter). Keep things manageable by limiting the terms you select to ones that are critical to understanding the content. Note that terms can be anything from people to places to symbols, abbreviations, or dates.

Example: A high school English teacher selected the following terms for a segment on sonnets: *sonnet*, *rhyme scheme*, *iambic pentameter*, *quatrain*, *couplet*, *Shakespeare*, and *Petrarch*.

Example: A US government teacher selected the following terms as part of a unit on the lawmaking process: *legislate*, *lobby*, *enact*, *vote*, *campaign*, *debate*, *override*, *compromise*, *filibuster*, and *amend*.

Ideas for getting students to engage with, use, and demonstrate their knowledge of word-wall terms:

- Play "use it or lose it" (students can play on their own or as part of a team). Award points for using word-wall terms in conversations, in written assignments, and/or on tests. The student (or team) with the most points at the end of a specified time period wins.
- Play "missed opportunity." Give students buzzers. Encourage them to buzz any time there's a missed word-wall opportunity (a place where you or a classmate could've used a word-wall term to express an idea more precisely but didn't). Have them explain what the term is and how it could have been used to express the original speaker's idea more precisely.
- Invite students to define word-wall terms using the method(s) of their choice. Possibilities include crafting original and student-friendly definitions, listing critical attributes, developing similes or sketches that capture meaning, or making/explaining connections to other words on the wall.
- Require students to use a specific number of word-wall terms when completing a written assignment or test question. ("In order to get full credit, you must include three word-wall terms.")
- Challenge students to incorporate as many terms as possible into a story, summary, or other piece of writing. See the Vocabulary Storytellers tool (pp. 123–125) for ideas and examples.
- Develop and test students' understanding of how terms/concepts relate to one another (L.CCR.5) by asking them to explain the connection between two or more terms (e.g., "a *pulley* is a type of *simple machine*," "a *chick* is a baby *bird*," or "*weight-bearing activities*, like *jogging* and *dancing*, develop *bone strength*").
- When appropriate, encourage students to explore the ways that word-wall terms are used outside your particular discipline (e.g., a "magnetic personality" vs. "magnetic" in a science context).
- Invite students to illustrate the meanings of word-wall terms. Post the sketches that best capture the terms' meanings on the word wall. (Note that using visuals to clarify ideas/information is consistent with the goals of Common Core SL.CCR.5 and W.CCR.2.)

Transitional Word Walls

Description/Purpose:

Transitional word walls familiarize students with linking and organizing words like *first*, *after that*, *in contrast*, and *as a result.*

How these word walls develop the 3Cs:

Making students aware of transitional words and their functions prepares them to better **C**omprehend the structure and meaning of assigned texts. Encouraging students to use these words when speaking and writing helps them **C**ommunicate in the kind of clear and coherent way that the **C**ommon Core State Standards (W.CCR.1–4, SL.CCR.4) demand.

Creating your wall:

Select transitional words that are both age appropriate and consistent with the type(s) of writing tasks you'll be focusing on in class. See The Missing Links tool (p. 77, specifically) for a list of options to choose from.

Example: *First*, *next*, *then*, *after that*, and *finally* would be good choices for writing tasks that involve describing a series of steps or events.

Example: *On the contrary, on the other hand, conversely,* and *alternatively* would be good choices for writing tasks that involve presenting contrasting viewpoints.

Ideas for getting students to engage with, use, and demonstrate their knowledge of word-wall terms:

- Write (or have students write) a piece that includes at least five word-wall terms. Erase the word-wall terms, replace them with blank lines, and challenge students to fill in the blanks with appropriate terms. Review students' choices as a class. Highlight the idea that different words can be correct (e.g., you could introduce the second event in a sequence with *second*, *next*, *then*, or *after that*).
- Challenge students to include word-wall terms in an explanation, summary, argument/opinion piece, lab report, or narrative. Have them underline the terms for easy finding.

  Example (explanation): *First, I subtracted two from both sides of the equation. Then…*

  Example (argument piece): *Whereas some might argue that this kind of art has no place in…*

  Example (lab report): *For this reason, we decided to check the pH of our solution. Since it was low…*

  Example (narrative): *All in all, it was a great experience.*
- Give students samples of a specific type of writing piece (e.g., sequence, cause/effect, comparison). Have them underline the linking words and discuss the role that these words play in the overall structure and organization of this type of piece. Were the linking words used to connect a series of events? (*first, next, after that*) Present an outcome? (*as a result, consequently, thus*) Highlight similarities? (*similarly, in the same way, likewise*)
- Help students explore the different kinds of linking words that exist by having them organize a collection of these words into functional categories and give each category a descriptive label (e.g., *comparison words, order words, clarification words*). See p. 77 for some sample groupings.

Descriptive Word Walls

Description/Purpose:

Descriptive word walls expose students to the kinds of "awesome adjectives" and "va-va-voom verbs" that experts use to make their writing vivid, specific, and interesting.

How these word walls develop the 3Cs:

These word walls help students develop the "rich and varied vocabulary" that the **C**ommon Core ELA/Literacy Standards call for (Appendix A, p. 32; Language Standard 6). As such, they empower students both to **C**omprehend complex texts (R.CCR.10) and **C**ommunicate in ways that meet the standards' demands for precise language and descriptive details (W.CCR.2–3, SL.CCR.4, L.CCR.3).

Creating your wall:

Whenever possible, select verbs and adjectives (add adverbs if you want) that you can connect to a topic, theme, or text you're covering in class. Choosing words that are linked to your content in some way will make the words easier for you and your students to use in classroom conversations and writing assignments. It also gives the words context, which can make them more meaningful and memorable for students.

Example: A primary-grade teacher used a Halloween-themed unit to introduce this group of interesting verbs and adjectives: *spook, howl, screech, petrified, eerie.*

Example: A social studies teacher created a descriptive word wall around her Age of Exploration unit by selecting verbs and adjectives that described the explorers (*resolute, daring, bold, weather-beaten*), the things they did (*embark, navigate, persist, subjugate*), and their journeys (*arduous, interminable, treacherous, fortuitous*).

Example: A math teacher prepared students to describe data trends on charts and graphs more precisely by posting these words on her wall: *rise, drop, climb, plateau, gradual, steady, steep, sharp, dramatic, mild.*

Note: While the words on this kind of wall can have connections to the content that students are studying, they shouldn't be specific to that content or content area. Instead, they should be general terms that students would likely encounter in a wide range of texts and contexts (i.e., the "general academic" or "Tier 2" terms referred to in both Language Standard 6 and Appendix A from the Common Core ELA/Literacy Standards).

Ideas for getting students to engage with, use, and demonstrate their knowledge of word-wall terms:

- Challenge students to make an existing piece of writing (theirs, yours, or a published sample) more interesting and/or precise by replacing some of the existing words with word-wall terms.
- Encourage students to expand their vocabularies by finding and posting synonyms for word-wall terms.
- Target Common Core Language Standard 5 by helping students explore subtle differences between related words. In the Halloween-themed wall described above, for example, you might discuss the similarities and differences between *screeching* and *howling* (both involve loud sounds, but not equivalent ones).
- Another way to target Language Standard 5: Ask students to show their grasp of the terms by relating them to their opposites (antonyms) and to words with similar but not identical meanings (synonyms).
- Challenge students to include a specific number of word-wall terms in a description, summary, explanation, or narrative. Have them underline the terms for easy finding/counting.
- Create a fill-in-the-blank piece that students can complete using word-wall terms. Discuss it as a class.
- Have students find real-world or literary examples of the terms (e.g., animals that are *furry*, stories that are *inspiring*, characters who are *courageous*, or athletes who *persevere* through challenges).

"Task & Test Verb" Word Walls

Description/Purpose:

Task & Test Verb word walls feature the types of thinking and test-taking verbs that appear in task descriptions, test questions, and standards documents—verbs like *compare*, *calculate*, *explain*, and *analyze*.

How these word walls develop the 3Cs:

These word walls familiarize students with verbs they're likely to encounter on standards-based test questions—for example, questions that are aligned with the Common Core State Standards or Next Generation Science Standards. Familiarizing students with these verbs prepares them to Comprehend these questions more easily and Communicate appropriate responses (i.e., responses that both address the question and reflect their understanding of the relevant material).

Creating your wall:

Select verbs that reflect the demands of standards documents and standards-based assessment tests. (A list of possibilities is provided on p. 122.) You can select your verbs at random, go in order from most to least used (which verbs appear most frequently in the standards for your particular grade level?), or pick verbs that reflect the thinking demands, assessment tasks, and test questions associated with an upcoming instructional unit. Regardless of how you choose your verbs, be selective. Focus on a few at a time so that students can learn them deeply.

Example: If lesson plans call for students to *observe* plants and animals so as to *compare* the diversity of life in different habitats (Next Generation Science Standard 2-LS4-1), you might put the terms *observe* and *compare* on your word wall.

Example: Prepare students for computerized assessment tests by familarizing them with words like *scroll*, *click*, *drag and drop*, and *highlight*.

Note: Remember to teach thinking and test-taking terms in the same way you'd teach "regular" vocabulary terms—by defining, modeling, giving examples, and checking for understanding. For more on how to teach and define these particular kinds of terms, see the Task & Test Verbs tool, pp. 120–122.

Ideas for getting students to engage with, use, and demonstrate their knowledge of word-wall terms:

- Encourage students to define the terms using language that makes sense to them. Examples of student-friendly definitions can be found in the Task & Test Verbs tool (see the table on p. 121).
- Have students compare and contrast potentially confusing terms (e.g., "What's the difference between *persuading* and *arguing*?" or "What's the difference between *estimating* and *calculating*?").
- Generate questions/tasks that include word-wall terms in the instructions (e.g., "*Compare* the two accounts of this event"). Use students' responses to evaluate their understanding of the terms in question (e.g., did they actually *compare* the two accounts when writing their responses?). Redefine and review any terms that students are unclear about.
- Invite students to generate study questions that include word-wall terms. Have them respond to their own questions, exchange questions with a partner, or submit their questions to you for possible inclusion on a future test.
- Let students "play teacher." Find (or generate) an incorrect response to a short-answer question that can be traced to a "task-or-test-verb misunderstanding." Have students identify and explain where the test-taker went wrong. ("The question asked you to *compare* velocity and acceleration, but all you did was *describe* them. To *compare*, you would've had to explain how they were similar and different.")

Concept Definition Map

What is it?

A visual framework (adapted from Schwartz & Raphael, 1985) that helps students define and deepen their grasp of key terms/concepts

What are the benefits of using this tool?

Asking students to define key terms in their own words can be an effective vocabulary-building strategy. In order for this strategy to work, however, students must know *how* to craft meaningful definitions—and that's not something we often teach them. This tool corrects the problem by giving students a simple strategy for generating deep and detailed definitions of critical terms and concepts. Students map out the key components using a simple visual organizer, and then use those components to develop their definitions. The process as a whole addresses key elements of Common Core Language Standards 4–6.

What are the basic steps?

1. Talk to students about the value of understanding critical terms/concepts. Clarify that the goal of today's lesson is to teach them a strategy that can help them define and deepen their understanding of these terms/concepts.

2. Explain that the first step in the strategy involves looking for four kinds of information about whatever term they're trying to define (a Concept Definition Map, p. 119, has a place for each):
   - A larger category that the term fits into
   - Other items that belong in that same category
   - The term's key attributes, especially ones that distinguish it from other items in the category
   - Examples of the term

3. Model the process of completing a Concept Definition Map using a familiar term like *bicycle*. Help students use the information from the completed map to generate a deep and detailed definition of the selected term.

4. Ask students to think about the kinds of resources that could help them complete a map for a less familiar, or completely unfamiliar, term.

   Possible responses: dictionary, encyclopedia, Internet, lecture/lesson, textbook, prior knowledge

5. Guide students through the process of completing a map for an unfamiliar term (e.g., a bold-faced term from a textbook). Give them time to search appropriate resources, and have them use their maps to generate deep and detailed definitions. Offer assistance and feedback as needed.

6. Ask students to use the Concept Definition Map technique independently, either with terms that you select for them or terms they select themselves. In either case, confirm that the selected terms are both appropriate for the Concept Definition Map format and worth defining in detail.

How is this tool used in the classroom?

- ✔ To help students deepen their understanding of critical terms/concepts
- ✔ To scaffold the process of developing rich and detailed definitions
- ✔ To teach students a vocabulary-building strategy that they can use independently

This tool can be used across grade levels and content areas. Map *square* in a primary-grade class, *jazz* in a music class, *democracy* in a history class, or *alkali metals* in a chemistry class. The chemistry map is available at www.ThoughtfulClassroom.com/Tools; other maps are shown below.

EXAMPLE 1: Secondary ELA

In preparation for a courage-themed literature unit, a teacher asked students to use their background knowledge and whatever other sources they wanted to map and define the term *courage*. At the end of the unit, they were encouraged to revisit and refine their initial definitions.

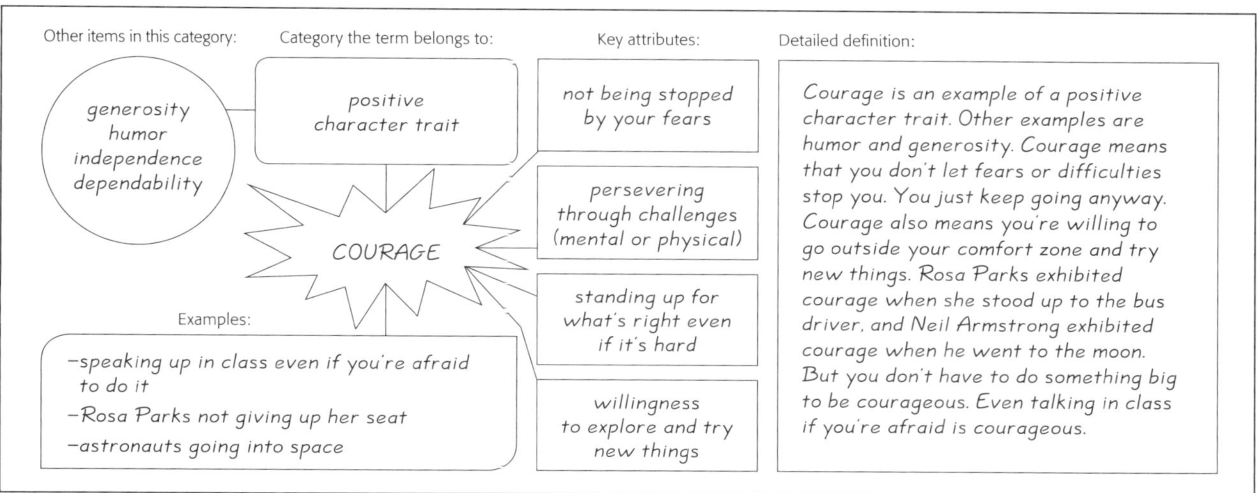

EXAMPLE 2: Elementary mathematics

To help her students recognize that different tools have different purposes and properties, an elementary teacher had them explore a variety of measuring tools and complete a Concept Definition Map for each one. Her big-picture goal was to develop students' ability to select the appropriate tool for a given task (Common Core Mathematical Practice 5).

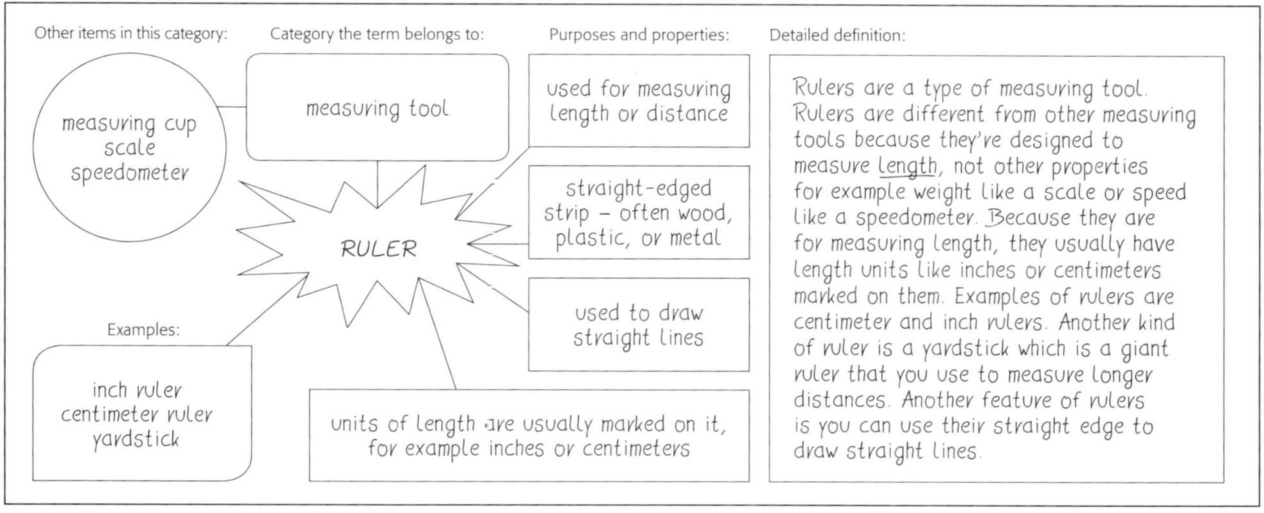

Teacher Talk

➔ Here are some scaffolding suggestions:

- Have students complete Concept Definition Maps as a class (or in pairs/small groups) rather than individually. Provide guidance and assistance as needed.
- Before having students generate Concept Definition Maps from scratch, help them gain a better understanding of the overall format and components by selecting a term, recording the elements that a completed map would contain on slips of paper (three example slips, one big-category slip, etc.), and having students paste those slips in the appropriate places on a blank map. Review their completed maps as a class.
- Instead of requiring students to seek out resources on their own, provide them with a packet of materials to choose from (e.g., a clipped-out dictionary definition, an encyclopedia entry, a relevant textbook passage, some photos, and a glossary entry).

➔ Feel free to adjust the basic map format. Among other things, you might add boxes for recording uses/applications, pros/cons, synonyms/antonyms, or the big-picture significance of the concept being investigated.

➔ Encourage students to apply what they learn from this technique to defining important terms in general. ("Whenever you're trying to define a key term or concept, picture the components of a definition that appear on a Concept Definition Map, and include as many of those components as possible in your definition.")

➔ Clarify that it's not necessary to learn *all* words in this amount of detail. Think (and ask students to think) about criteria that could be used to decide which words are worth mapping.

➔ This tool has ties to a number of Common Core Language Standards.

- It addresses Standard 4 by inviting students to determine (or clarify) the meanings of unknown words using appropriate reference materials.
- It addresses Standard 5 both by having students define words by category and key attributes, and by having students explore item/category relationships.
- It addresses Standard 6 by helping students acquire new vocabulary knowledge.

Name: Date:

Concept Definition Map

Other items in this category:

Catego·y the term belongs to:

Key attributes:

Examples:

Detailed definition:

Note: This framework is adapted from the work of Schwartz and Raphael (1985).

Task & Test Verbs

What is it?

A vocabulary-building tool that targets the kinds of verbs students are likely to see on today's assessment tests—verbs like *analyze*, *evaluate*, *compare*, and *support*

What are the benefits of using this tool?

Students can't complete tasks and test questions successfully unless they understand the directions. (This point is beautifully illustrated by Heidi Hayes Jacobs's [2006] anecdote about students who thought that "drawing conclusions" meant sketching them.) This tool, which was inspired by Jacobs's ideas on the importance of helping students "translate the directions," prepares students for success by teaching them the meanings of verbs they're likely to encounter in task and test prompts. The focus is on verbs that reflect the demands of the Common Core ELA/Literacy Standards, the Common Core Mathematics Standards, and the Next Generation Science Standards.

What are the basic steps?

1. Skim the list of Task & Test Verbs on p. 122.
2. Decide which verbs are the most important for your students to know. Use your standards documents and sample assessment test items to help you make this decision.

   Example: If you skim the Common Core ELA/Literacy Standards, you'll see that first graders do need to know how to *retell* and *describe*, but aren't yet expected to *synthesize* or *evaluate*.
3. Choose a few key verbs to focus on. You can come back to the others later in the year.
4. Work with students to generate student-friendly definitions of the selected verbs. Definitions should take the following format: "If I am asked to ____, it means I should ____."

   Tip: Spend extra time on verbs like *draw* that can be used in multiple ways (e.g., *draw on* specific details from a text vs. *draw* an inference). Explain and model the different uses of these verbs.
5. Create sample tasks that include the selected verbs and complete them as a class. The idea is to model the thinking processes and behaviors that these verbs require.
6. Deepen and test students' understanding of the selected verbs. Among other things, you might
   - Have students create a Task & Test Verbs glossary or set of flashcards that they can use to practice and test their own (and their classmates') ability to define the selected verbs.
   - Use the verbs in classroom conversations. ("Do we agree that this passage *supports* Joe's claim?") Encourage students to do the same. ("Our group *analyzed* the data to see whether…")
   - Challenge students to complete sample tasks independently. Use their responses to evaluate their grasp of the verbs in question. Review or reteach any verbs that students are unclear about.

How is this tool used in the classroom?

- ✔ To familiarize students with the meanings of critical thinking and test-taking verbs
- ✔ To prepare students to understand and respond appropriately to test questions and tasks

EXAMPLES: Sample verbs reflecting different content areas and grade levels are shown below, along with their student-friendly translations.

Verb	Student-friendly definition
Retell	If I am asked to *retell* something, it means I should tell it again in my own words.
Classify	If I am asked to *classify* some things, it means I should organize them into groups based on some property like what shape they are, what kind of animal they are, or how they taste.
Evaluate	If I am asked to *evaluate* something, it means I should judge the merit or quality of that thing in a thoughtful way. I could be given specific criteria to use or asked to come up with my own.
Draw a conclusion	If I am asked to *draw* a conclusion, it means I should make a conclusion based on the given evidence or information.
Draw on details from a text	If I am asked to *draw on* details from a text, it means I should include details from the text in my answer. This can be actual quotations or just specific ideas or information I saw in the text.

Teacher Talk

➔ Before deciding to skip a verb whose meaning seems obvious (something like *compare*), confirm that the meaning of that verb is as clear to students as it is to you. You may be surprised!

Tip: You can determine which verbs need teaching by administering a pretest. (Can students define the verbs in their own words? Respond successfully to prompts that include them? If not, put those verbs on the to-do list.) Differentiate instruction as needed.

➔ Prepare students for computer-based assessment tests by teaching (and testing their ability to execute) computer-command verbs like *click*, *highlight*, *scroll*, *select*, and *drag and drop*.

➔ The list on p. 122 includes verbs that commonly appear in task and test prompts. Some of these verbs describe actions that students need to take (e.g., *retell* a passage or *support* a claim with evidence); others appear in different contexts. The verb *develop*, for example, might appear in a question that asks students to explain how an author *develops* a specific theme.

➔ Adjust the definition format in Step 4 to fit the verbs you select and the way that they're used. With verbs like *influenced*, *developed*, or *contributed to*, for example, you might try something like this: "If I am asked how someone/something __ something else, I should __." ("If I am asked how something *influenced* something else, I should say how the first thing affected the second thing.")

Note: You can also have students define a verb in a specific context (e.g., have them explain what it means to "address a counterargument" rather than having them define *address* in a general sense).

➔ For more on the vocabulary-building approaches discussed in this tool, as well as additional tips and strategies, check out Robert Marzano's (2004) *Building Background Knowledge for Academic Achievement* or Marilee Sprenger's (2013) "11 Tips on Teaching Common Core Critical Vocabulary."

Task & Test Verbs

Acknowledge	**Develop**	Organize
Add to	Distinguish	Paraphrase
Address	**Drag/Drag and drop**	Predict
Analyze	**Draw/Draw on**	Prove
Apply	Edit	Provide
Articulate	**Elaborate**	Quote
Assess	Eliminate	Recount
Build/Build on	Emphasize	**Refer to/Reference**
Calculate	Estimate	Relate
Cite	**Evaluate**	Represent
Clarify	**Explain**	Retell
Classify	Express	Reveal
Click	Generate	Review
Compare	Graph	Revise
Complete	Highlight	Round
Conclude	Identify	Select
Consult	Illustrate	Solve
Contrast	Imply	Specify
Contribute to	Infer	**State/Restate**
Critique	Influence	Suggest
Defend	**Integrate**	**Summarize**
Define	**Interpret**	Supply
Delineate	Introduce	**Support**
Demonstrate	**Justify**	**Synthesize**
Describe	Locate	Trace
Determine	Measure	Verify

Note: This list was generated following an analysis of the Common Core State Standards, the Next Generation Science Standards, sample test items from the PARCC and Smarter Balanced Assessment Consortiums, and sample tasks from Appendix B of the ELA/Literacy Standards. Feel free to revise it to reflect your specific standards documents. The twenty verbs that we believe are the most critical to know are in marked in bold.

Vocabulary Storytellers

What is it?

A tool that tests students' command of critical vocabulary terms by challenging them to incorporate those terms into a story

What are the benefits of using this tool?

We often test students' vocabulary knowledge by asking them to define specific terms or match those terms to their corresponding definitions. The problem with these approaches is that they don't tell us whether students can actually *use* the vocabulary terms they've learned (a goal of Common Core Language Standard 6) or whether they've simply memorized a series of definitions. This tool, which challenges students to incorporate key terms into an original story, provides a deeper, more authentic, and more engaging way to assess vocabulary knowledge.

What are the basic steps?

1. Before beginning a lesson or unit, identify the critical vocabulary terms/concepts that students will need to know and understand.

2. Share the list of terms with students before instruction begins. Help them monitor and improve their understanding of these terms throughout the course of instruction.

3. At the end of the lesson or unit, ask students to demonstrate their understanding of some or all of the key terms by incorporating them into an original story (terms should be underlined).

4. Clarify the ground rules and assessment criteria before students begin working, and use specific examples (positive and negative) to help them understand what the task entails. For example:

- *Ground rules:* "Stories can take any format (e.g., fable, mystery, science fiction), be about any topic that interests you (e.g., friends, dinosaurs, current events), and be as long or short as you choose."
- *Assessment criteria:* "The only requirements are that you underline the terms you use and that you use those terms in a way that makes it clear you understand what they mean."
- *One example:* "On its own, a sentence like 'I love planets' would *not* satisfy the requirements of the task since it doesn't make it clear that you know anything about planets."

5. Evaluate students' work using the assessment criteria you established in Step 4: Are the relevant terms underlined? Have students demonstrated a clear understanding of those terms?

6. Work with students one-on-one or as a class to improve their understanding of any misused terms.

How is this tool used in the classroom?

✔ To test students' ability to understand and use critical vocabulary terms in context

✔ To have students synthesize and demonstrate their learning through writing

EXAMPLE 1: Secondary science

A biology student wrote this story at the end of a unit on cell structure and function:

> *Help!!!!! I'm not sure how this happened, but I've somehow been miniaturized and injected into someone else's body! Just last week, I was sitting in biology class learning about cells and how they're the building blocks of all living things—and today, I'm getting to see some firsthand. I actually just slid inside of one, so I guess I'm one of the substances that can pass through its semi-permeable outer membrane! Now that I'm inside, I'm floating in a gelatinous material known as the cytosol. All around me, I see different cellular structures called organelles, which are performing their unique cellular functions. This would actually be kind of cool except that I'm sensing a problem with the cell's power plants, which are technically called mitochondria. They seem to be having trouble generating enough adenosine triphosphate, and that could spell trouble since ATP is a critical source of energy...*

SOURCE: From *Tools for Thoughtful Assessment* (p. 171), by A. L. Boutz, H. F. Silver, J. W. Jackson, and M. J. Perini, 2012, Ho-Ho-Kus, NJ: Thoughtful Education Press. © 2012 by Silver Strong & Associates. Reprinted with permission.

EXAMPLE 2: Secondary mathematics

A high school math teacher challenged her students to demonstrate their understanding of the similarities and differences between linear and quadratic functions by writing a story. The beginning of one student's story is shown below; see www.ThoughtfulClassroom.com/Tools for the rest.

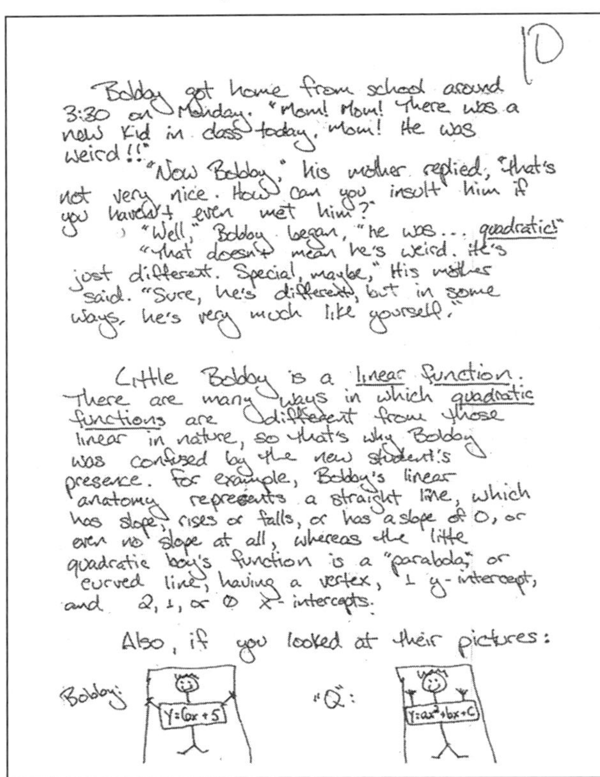

10

Bobby got home from school around 3:30 on Monday. "Mom! Mom! There was a new kid in class today, Mom! He was weird!!"

"Now Bobby," his mother replied, "that's not very nice. How can you insult him if you haven't even met him?"

"Well," Bobby began, "he was... quadratic!"

"That doesn't mean he's weird. He's just different. Special, maybe," his mother said. "Sure, he's different, but in some ways, he's very much like yourself."

Little Bobby is a linear function. There are many ways in which quadratic functions are different from those linear in nature, so that's why Bobby was confused by the new student's presence. For example, Bobby's linear anatomy represents a straight line, which has slope, rises or falls, or has a slope of 0, or even no slope at all, whereas the little quadratic boy's function is a "parabola" or curved line, having a vertex, 1 y-intercept, and 2, 1, or 0 x-intercepts.

Also, if you looked at their pictures:

Bobby: $y=6x+5$

"Q": $y=ax^2+bx+c$

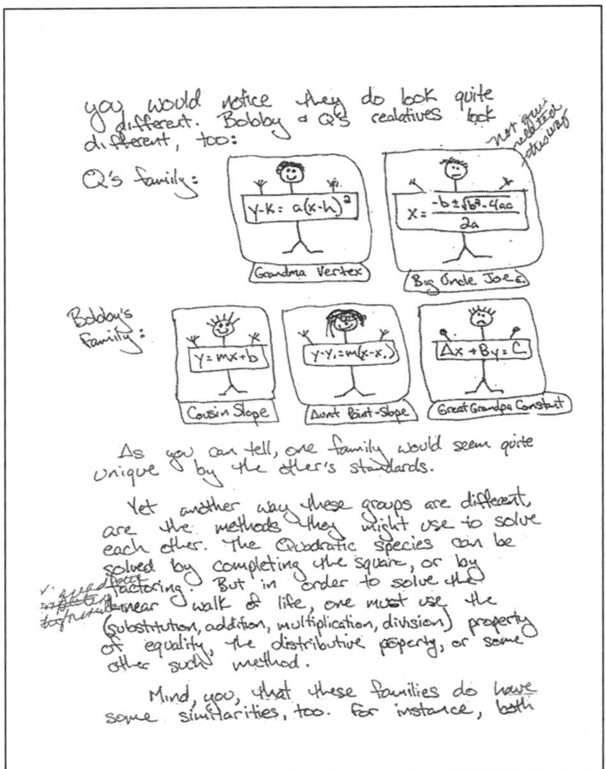

you would notice they do look quite different. Bobby & Q's relatives look different, too:

Q's family: $y-k=a(x-h)^2$ (Grandma Vertex); $x=\frac{-b\pm\sqrt{b^2-4ac}}{2a}$ (Big Uncle Joe)

Bobby's family: $y=mx+b$ (Cousin Slope); $y-y_1=m(x-x_1)$ (Aunt Point-Slope); $Ax+By=C$ (Great Grandpa Constant)

As you can tell, one family would seem quite unique by the other's standards.

Yet another way these groups are different are the methods they might use to solve each other. The Quadratic species can be solved by completing the square, or by factoring. But in order to solve the linear walk of life, one must use the (substitution, addition, multiplication, division) property of equality, the distributive property, or some other such method.

Mind you, that these families do have some similarities, too. For instance, both

SOURCE: From *Tools for Thoughtful Assessment* (p. 171), by A. L. Boutz, H. F. Silver, J. W. Jackson, and M. J. Perini, 2012, Ho-Ho-Kus, NJ: Thoughtful Education Press. © 2012 by Silver Strong & Associates. Reprinted with permission.

EXAMPLE 3: Primary mathematics

A kindergarten teacher tested students' ability to use shape terms to describe objects in their environment (Common Core K.G.A.1). To make the tool more age appropriate, she had students fill in the blanks in a story that she created (she read the story aloud; they shouted out answers).

> Shapes are all around us. When we enter the classroom each morning, we pass through a brown door that is a rectangle. We begin each day by sitting on an oval rug and listening to a story. We show which stories are our favorites by putting gold star stickers on them. After story time, we check the clock, which is a circle, to see if it's…

SOURCE: From *Tools for Thoughtful Assessment* (p. 171), by A. L. Boutz, H. F. Silver, J. W. Jackson, and M. J. Perini, 2012, Ho-Ho-Kus, NJ: Thoughtful Education Press. © 2012 by Silver Strong & Associates. Reprinted with permission.

Teacher Talk

➔ Feel free to modify the basic Vocabulary Storytellers format. Here are five other ways to check (and have students check) their ability to use critical vocabulary terms in context:

Option 1: Challenge students to incorporate a select number of vocabulary terms into a different kind of written piece. Rather than a story, for instance, have them write an editorial, a book review, a summary, or a letter. For example, "Write a letter to the president that expresses your thoughts and feelings about his State of the Union address. Include as many of this week's vocabulary terms as you can."

Option 2: Ask students to use critical vocabulary terms in an oral presentation (e.g., a debate, classroom discussion, or oral report) instead of a story. For example, "Prepare a sixty-second news report about the 2011 tsunami in Japan. Include at least six of the following ten terms in your report…" Use the change in format as an opportunity to teach and/or test Common Core presentation skills (see Speaking & Listening Standards 4–6).

Option 3: Give students a writing prompt and instruct them to include a specific number of terms in their responses. For example, "Use five of the words from our word wall in your response to this prompt: 'If you were Punxsutawney Phil, how would you feel on Groundhog Day?'"

Option 4: Ask students to write a story that highlights the similarities and differences between two specific terms. A creative example using linear and quadratic functions is shown on p. 124.

Option 5: Have students write a story as a class (pick students' names out of a hat to see who writes first, second, etc.). Student 1 picks a term and writes it into the opening sentence(s); Student 2 adds to the story, including another term; and the process continues until all terms have been used.

➔ Use the tool's story format as an opportunity to develop narrative writing skills (Common Core W.CCR.3) as well as content-specific vocabulary knowledge (L.CCR.6).

Word Arrays

What is it?

A tool that helps students visualize shades of meaning among sets of related words (part of Common Core Language Standard 5) by having them arrange those words on an array

What are the benefits of using this tool?

Fisher and Frey (2008) note that "subtle differences between related words can be very confusing for students" (p. 81). This tool uses a comparative approach to help students grasp these subtle differences. Students explore the definitions of related words, order those words along a continuum, and reflect on the impact of using one word over another. By getting students to reflect on shades of meaning, we not only improve their vocabularies, we also teach them to think more carefully about word choice when speaking and writing.

What are the basic steps?

1. Generate a list of related words (e.g., *toss, throw, hurl*). Record the words on the handout (p. 129), present the words to students, and identify the criteria that students should use to arrange the words on the array (e.g., "Arrange these words from most to least forceful").

Note: If students have some knowledge of the given words, they should generate a tentative array. Explain that it doesn't have to be correct; encourage them to use pencil in case of errors.

2. Instruct students to learn (or check their understanding of) each word's meaning by consulting one or more dictionaries. Have them use what they learn to generate student-friendly definitions (on their own or as a class) and record those definitions on the handout.

3. Have students use their definitions to arrange the words along the array. (Students who created tentative arrays in Step 1 should revise those arrays as needed.)

Tip: Model the process before asking students to do it independently. ("*Whispering* is the quietest way to say something, so I'll put it first. *Mumbling* is when you intentionally say something quietly so others can't hear, so I think that should go next. *Saying* is speaking in a normal tone, so…")

4. Develop and test students' understanding of the words on the array. See Teacher Talk for ideas.

5. Initiate a conversation about the reasons someone might want to use one "array word" rather than another. Word-choice scenarios like this one are a good way to get the ball rolling:

"If we were writing a story about a pitcher who was trying to strike out the batter he was pitching to, would he be more likely to *hurl* the ball toward the plate or *toss* it in? If our goal were to help a reader really picture the action, why might either of these two words be a better choice than *throw*?"

6. Encourage students to refer to their arrays when writing and revising. Remind them to choose their words thoughtfully rather than using the first words that come to mind. ("Review your draft. Can you replace any of the existing words with ones that are more vivid, accurate, or descriptive?")

How is this tool used in the classroom?

✔ To help students appreciate subtle differences between words with similar meanings
✔ To develop students' vocabularies, so they can express themselves more precisely
✔ To help students choose their words more thoughtfully and appreciate the choices of others

Word Arrays can be used across grade levels and content areas, as shown by these examples:

EXAMPLE 1: Primary

After acting out each of these "looking words" from Common Core Standard L.1.5d, a first-grade teacher helped students define and rank them by intensity:

EXAMPLE 2: ELA

A teacher used this tool to familiarize students with more vivid and descriptive alternatives for the overly used word *said*. She had them rank the alternatives by loudness level, and encouraged them to build these alternatives into their writing.

EXAMPLE 3: Science

A science teacher uses this tool on a regular basis to help her students develop the word knowledge they need to express their ideas with precision. Two of the arrays she had them generate are shown below. The first is a ranking of "temperature terms" from coldest to hottest; the second is a list of "knowing terms" from least to most certain.

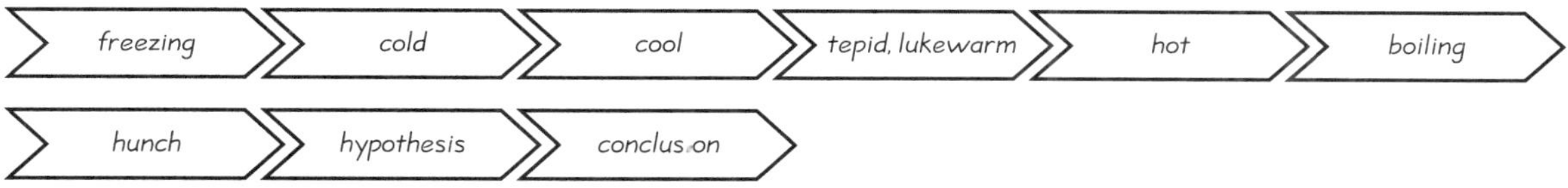

EXAMPLE 4: Elementary

An elementary teacher had students rank these "timing words" by frequency:

EXAMPLE 5: Music

A music teacher had students rank these "dynamics terms" by relative volume (softest to loudest):

EXAMPLE 6: Physical education

A physical education teacher familiarized kindergarten students with key locomotor skills/terms by helping them define, act out, and rank these terms from slowest to fastest:

Teacher Talk

➔ If pairs of words have almost identical meanings, it may be impossible to separate them on an array. The words *lukewarm* and *tepid*, for example, have such similar meanings that it would be hard to decide which goes where on a hottest-to-coolest array. Let students know that words like these can be placed in the same box rather than in adjacent boxes, as shown in Example 3.

➔ Here are two possible ways to reinforce/test students' grasp of the words on an array (Step 4):

- Ask students to complete this similarities-and-differences frame: "_____ and _____ are similar in that they both _____. They differ in that _____." (Example: "*Hurling* and *tossing* are similar in that they both refer to throwing something. They differ in that *hurling* is a lot more forceful than *tossing*.")
- Have students choose the appropriate word for a given scenario and explain their rationale. ("Read the paragraph. Given the context, which 'array word' would fit best in the blank? Why?")

➔ Looking for a fun extension activity? Challenge students to use a thesaurus to identify additional words with similar meanings and add them to their arrays.

➔ Help students improve their understanding of action words (e.g., *saunter, walk, dash*) by acting out the words' meanings, as described in Examples 1 and 6.

➔ This tool has obvious ties to a key component of Common Core Language Standard 5 (distinguishing shades of meaning among closely related words), but it develops skills from other standards as well:

- It helps students acquire and use new vocabulary words. (L.CCR.6)
- It prepares students to express their ideas and experiences more precisely. (L.CCR.3, W.CCR.3)
- It encourages students to improve their written work (W.CCR.5) by making better word choices.
- It has students determine the meanings of unknown words using appropriate reference materials. (L.CCR.4)

Name: Date:

Word Arrays

Word	Definition

Array

Word Detectives

What is it?

A tool that prepares students to comprehend complex texts independently (Common Core Reading Standard 10) by teaching them to sleuth out the meanings of unknown words and phrases using context clues (Language Standard 4, Reading Standard 4)

What are the benefits of using this tool?

Ask students how to find the definition of an unknown word, and they'll likely tell you to look in a dictionary. This tool encourages students to take a different approach—to *guess* the meanings of unknown words based on clues in the surrounding text. The tool prepares students to make these kinds of educated guesses by familiarizing them with common types of context clues, by modeling the guessing process for them, and by providing guided and independent practice. By requiring students to indicate which portion(s) of a text helped them generate their tentative definitions, it also develops the Common Core practice of supporting inferences with text-based evidence (Reading Standard 1).

What are the basic steps?

1. Explain that using a dictionary isn't the only way to figure out the meaning of an unknown word—that it's often possible to sleuth out meanings using context clues (i.e., bits of information in the text that, along with students' prior knowledge, can provide hints about a word's meaning).

2. Use concrete examples to familiarize students with the types of context clues they might encounter while reading (see p. 131 for ideas).

Note: The goal isn't to have students memorize the different kinds of clues, but rather to teach them that texts provide many different kinds of hints, and that they should use any information they can to help them guess a word's meaning.

3. Teach students where to look for context clues. Train them to "look both ways" (before and/or after the unknown word) and "look near and far" (since clues won't always appear in the same sentence as the unknown word, students should scan surrounding sentences as well).

4. Distribute copies of the Word Detectives handout. Two versions are available (pp. 135–136): One uses a multiple-choice format; the other challenges students to generate a definition from scratch.

Note: When using the multiple-choice version, insert four definitions for students to choose from.

5. Model the process of deciphering an unknown word's meaning by working through the handout. (Give students copies of the passage with the unknown word so they can follow along.) Think aloud as you work so students can see what the process entails.

6. Go through several more examples as a class (new words/passages, new handouts).

7. Have students work through additional examples in pairs or small groups (observe and offer guidance). Determine whether additional instruction/modeling is needed or whether students are ready for independent practice.

Common Types of Context Clues

Definition clue: The unknown word is clearly and specifically defined right in the text—often in the same sentence as the unknown word. EXAMPLE: These drugs are **depressants**, substances that decrease the activity of the central nervous system. EXPLANATION: The unknown word ("depressants") is directly followed by its definition.
Visual clue: A picture or other image provides clues as to the meaning of the unknown word. EXAMPLE: On page 7 of *The Fire Cat*, we learn that "Pickles lives in a **barrel**." EXPLANATION: Since the key characteristics of a barrel are visible in the illustration that accompanies the text, students can use the illustration to generate a tentative definition (a hollow, cylinder-shaped container that bulges out a bit in the middle).
Description/explanation clue: A description or explanation that helps you understand the unknown word is provided in the text. EXAMPLE: "He was a very **restless** gentleman, sir, a-walkin' and a-stampin' all the time he was here." EXPLANATION: The description of the "restless gentleman" that's provided in the second half of the sentence (as someone who was constantly walking and stamping about) suggests that a restless person is someone who can't keep still.
Synonym clue: A nearby word (or phrase) with a similar but familiar meaning tips you off to the meaning of the unknown word. EXAMPLE: "It quoted Benjamin Franklin in 1789, a year before he died. He was too sick at the time to stand the shocks and bumps of any form of travel. 'I wish I had brought with me from France,' [he] said, 'a balloon sufficiently large to raise me from the ground. In my **malady**, it would be the most easy carriage for me…'" EXPLANATION: The word *sick* (two sentences before the unknown word) suggests that *malady* might mean illness.
Antonym/contrast clue: A nearby antonym or contrast helps you understand the meaning of the unknown word. (Words like *but*, *while*, *whereas*, *unlike*, *on the other hand*, *in contrast*, and *as opposed to* can often signal an antonym/contrast clue.) EXAMPLE: The chorionic membrane allows oxygen to enter and carbon dioxide to leave, but it's **impermeable** to water. EXPLANATION: The word *but* signals a contrast. The first part of the sentence says that oxygen and carbon dioxide can pass through the membrane. The *but* suggests that the opposite would be true for water—in other words, that water can't pass through it. Therefore, students might guess that *impermeable* means not allowing something to pass through it.
Example clue: Examples of the unknown word or phrase provide clues about meaning. EXAMPLE: **Capsaicin**-containing foods, like jalapeño and habanero peppers, are too much for me to handle! EXPLANATION: The fact that jalapeño and habanero peppers are examples of hot peppers suggests that *capsaicin* might be some kind of compound that gives peppers their hotness.
Inference clue: Even when none of the above types of clues exist, you can often use information in the surrounding text to infer the meaning of the unknown word. EXAMPLE: "Babar is riding happily on his mother's back when a **wicked** hunter, hidden behind some bushes, shoots at them. The hunter has killed Babar's mother!" EXPLANATION: The hunter's actions (he shoots and kills Babar's mother) should help students guess that a *wicked* person is someone who is mean or evil.

Note: The quoted passages in the second, third, fourth, and seventh examples are from Esther Averill's (1960/1983) *The Fire Cat*, p. 7; Arthur Conan Doyle's (1892–1893/1976) *The Original Illustrated Sherlock Holmes*, p. 214; William Pene du Bois's (1947/1986) *The Twenty-One Balloons*, p. 26; and Jean de Brunhoff's (1933/1937) *The Story of Babar*, pp. 6–7, respectively.

How is this tool used in the classroom?

✔ To help students determine the meanings of unknown words using context clues

✔ To have students use appropriate reference materials to check or clarify word meanings

EXAMPLE 1: Primary

A first-grade teacher encourages students to use visual clues to help them figure out the meanings of new vocabulary words during story time. While reading *Wiggling Worms at Work* (Pfeffer, 2003), for example, he challenged them to figure out the meaning of the verb *tunnel* just by looking at the picture—and they had no problem coming up with a tentative (and surprisingly accurate!) definition: to dig a path under the ground.

EXAMPLE 2: Elementary (modeling example)

A fifth-grade teacher uses passages from books that she and her students are reading to model the process of using context clues to decipher word meanings. Here, she explains how a contrast between the first and second parts of a sentence from Frances Hodgson Burnett's (1911/2008) *The Secret Garden* (see box below) helped her generate a tentative definition of the word *cease*:

"The sentence says that Mary had begun to be sorry for Mr. Craven, but then she started to *cease* being sorry for him. It sounds like her attitude toward Mr. Craven has changed, so maybe the idea is that she used to be sorry for him but no longer feels sorry for him now. So maybe *cease* means *stop*. If we replace the word *cease* with *stop*, does the sentence make sense? I think it does. It says that Mary started to think he deserved the bad things that had happened to him, and if she felt that way, she would stop feeling sorry. Let's check a dictionary to see if *cease* does in fact mean *stop*…"

> "Just as suddenly as she had begun to be rather sorry for Mr Archibald Craven, she began to **cease** to be sorry and to think he was unpleasant enough to deserve all that had happened to him" (p. 19).

EXAMPLE 3: Secondary (modeling example)

A high school teacher used a *Scientific American* article (Fischetti, 2007; see boxed excerpt below) to show students how context clues can help, even with scary-looking passages that are full of technical terms. He started by thinking aloud as he worked through the meaning of *traction control*:

"Does the author give us any clues? Hmm…It looks like he describes what a traction-control valve does (description/explanation clue) in that very same sentence! He says that it helps a spinning drive wheel grip the road. Since a traction-control valve is something that helps a wheel grip the road, I'm going to guess that *traction control* involves improving the grip of a tire on the road. Let's Google the phrase 'traction control' to see if my guess is on target…"

> "When a driver jams the brake pedal too hard, anti-lock hydraulic valves subtract brake pressure at a given wheel so the wheel does not lock up. As these systems proliferated in the 1990s, manufacturers tacked on **traction-control** valves that help a spinning drive wheel grip the road" (p. 96).

EXAMPLE 4: Elementary

Fourth graders were asked to try and figure out the meaning of the word *intruder* as it appeared in the following passage from *Owen & Mzee: The True Story of a Remarkable Friendship* (Hatkoff, Hatkoff, & Kahumbu, 2011):

> "They called Haller Park, an animal sanctuary about fifty miles away, near the city of Mombasa. Dr. Paula Kahumbu, the manager, immediately offered Owen a place to live there. She explained that he could never be returned to the wild. Since he was still a baby, he wouldn't have learned yet how to fend for himself. And he would never be welcomed into another hippo pod—he would be seen as an **intruder** and attacked" (p. 614).

One student's work is shown below.

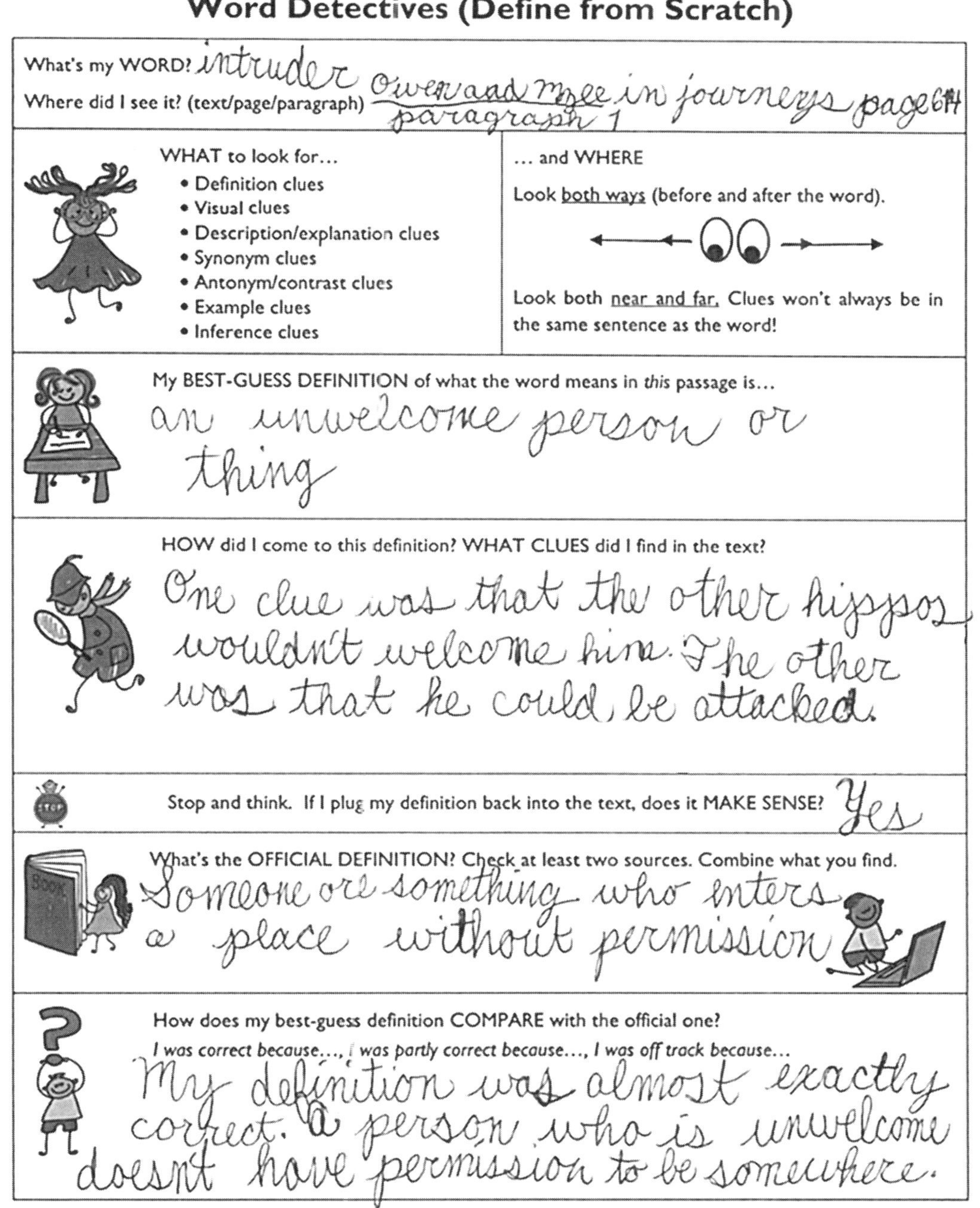

Word Detectives (Define from Scratch)

What's my WORD? intruder

Where did I see it? (text/page/paragraph) Owen and Mzee in journeys page 614 paragraph 1

WHAT to look for...
- Definition clues
- Visual clues
- Description/explanation clues
- Synonym clues
- Antonym/contrast clues
- Example clues
- Inference clues

... and WHERE

Look both ways (before and after the word).

Look both near and far. Clues won't always be in the same sentence as the word!

My BEST-GUESS DEFINITION of what the word means in *this* passage is...
an unwelcome person or thing

HOW did I come to this definition? WHAT CLUES did I find in the text?
One clue was that the other hippos wouldn't welcome him. The other was that he could be attacked.

Stop and think. If I plug my definition back into the text, does it MAKE SENSE? Yes

What's the OFFICIAL DEFINITION? Check at least two sources. Combine what you find.
Someone ore something who enters a place without permission

How does my best-guess definition COMPARE with the official one?
I was correct because..., I was partly correct because..., I was off track because...
My definition was almost exactly correct. a person who is unwelcome doesn't have permission to be somewhere.

Teacher Talk

➔ Clarify that students won't always be able to guess a word's meaning—or guess it perfectly—from context clues alone, but that they can often get close enough to make sense of what they've read.

➔ Teach students to explain and support their best-guess definitions using specific words and details from the text. Supporting responses with text-based evidence is a key Common Core skill.

➔ Help students get comfortable with the process of using context clues to decipher word meanings by having them sleuth out the meanings of words from single sentences rather than complex text passages. You can create sentences with obvious clues expressly for this purpose.

➔ Remind students that words can have multiple meanings—and that their goal is to decipher the meaning of a word in context (i.e., what does it mean in the given passage?). Reinforce the importance of checking that their definition makes sense *in the given passage* (a step on the handout).

➔ Encourage students to consult multiple dictionaries (or other reference materials) before recording an official definition. Have them use what they learn to generate their own definitions rather than copying a definition from a single source. Reviewing definitions from multiple sources helps students understand words more completely and accurately, and generating their own definitions rather than copying existing ones facilitates retention.

Another option: Because "dictionary language" can be confusing, you may want to create official definitions as a class. The definitions you generate should be written in student-friendly language.

➔ Clarify that using context clues is a strategy that students should use independently, whether they're reading for pleasure, for other classes, or a standardized exam. Teaching students strategies for deciphering the meanings of unknown words is a great way to develop the "independence in gathering vocabulary knowledge" that's required by the Common Core State Standards (L.CCR.6). And having this ability prepares students to comprehend complex texts independently (R.CCR.10).

➔ Help students expand their vocabularies (Common Core L.CCR.6) by developing follow-up activities that deepen and reinforce their grasp of the words whose meanings they sleuthed out.

➔ Explain that analyzing word parts (roots, prefixes, suffixes) is another way that students can use what *they* know (rather than a dictionary) to try and figure out the meanings of unknown words. Help students remember to consider both word parts *and* context clues by training them to search for hints both "inside and outside" unknown words (Fisher & Frey, 2013).

➔ Context clues can help students sleuth out the meanings of nonliteral as well as literal words and phrases. In Martin Luther King, Jr.'s 1963 "Letter from Birmingham Jail," for example, the sentences surrounding the phrase "a single garment of destiny" provide hints as to the meaning of that phrase.

> "Injustice anywhere is a threat to justice everywhere. We are caught in an inescapable network of mutuality, tied in **a single garment of destiny**. Whatever affects one directly affects all indirectly" (King, 2003, p. 85).

➔ Encouraging students to look for visual clues (see Example 1) teaches them to use images as a means of understanding what they're reading—a goal of Common Core Reading Standard 7.

Name: Date:

Word Detectives: Multiple-Choice Format

What's my WORD?

Where did I see it? (text/page/paragraph)

WHAT to look for…

- Definition clues
- Visual clues
- Description/explanation clues
- Synonym clues
- Antonym/contrast clues
- Example clues
- Inference clues

… and WHERE

Look both ways (before and after the word).

Look both near and far. Clues won't always be in the same sentence as the word!

What does the word mean in this passage? My BEST GUESS is…

a)

b)

c)

d)

HOW did I come to this definition? WHAT CLUES did I find in the text?

Stop and think. If I plug my definition back into the text, does it MAKE SENSE?

What's the OFFICIAL DEFINITION? Check at least two sources. Combine what you find.

Was my initial guess CORRECT? _________

If not, can I find anything now that supports the correct definition?

Name: Date:

Word Detectives: Define from Scratch

What's my WORD?
Where did I see it? (text/page/paragraph)

WHAT to look for...

- Definition clues
- Visual clues
- Description/explanation clues
- Synonym clues
- Antonym/contrast clues
- Example clues
- Inference clues

... and WHERE

Look both ways (before and after the word).

Look both near and far. Clues won't always be in the same sentence as the word!

My BEST-GUESS DEFINITION of what the word means in this passage is...

HOW did I come to this definition? WHAT CLUES did I find in the text?

Stop and think. If I plug my definition back into the text, does it MAKE SENSE?

What's the OFFICIAL DEFINITION? Check at least two sources. Combine what you find.

How does my best-guess definition COMPARE with the official one?
I was correct because... I was partly correct because... I was off track because...

You Be the Teacher

What is it?

A tool that tests students' command of Common Core (or other) skills by having them check and correct papers—just like a teacher!

What are the benefits of using this tool?

Many students we've worked with, even the older ones, love correcting papers. This tool capitalizes on students' fondness for playing teacher by inviting them to review pieces of work, find the errors, and make the appropriate corrections. Besides being fun, having students identify and correct errors provides valuable feedback about their understanding of the relevant material and good practice for fix-the-errors-type test items. Because the samples of work that students correct are teacher-generated, they can be designed to test students' grasp of whatever skills you're working on at the time—anything from punctuating sentences properly to adding and subtracting mixed numbers.

What are the basic steps?

1. Identify a skill (or set of related skills) that you've been working to develop.
2. Create a sample piece of work that contains the kinds of errors students might make if they *didn't* have a good grasp of the skill(s) in question.
3. Give students copies of the sample piece you generated. Tell them that you want them to play teacher and review this piece of work. Explain that they need to find and correct all the errors.
4. Examine students' work to see if they found all the errors and fixed them correctly. Use what you learn to determine which students have mastered the skill(s) you were testing and which need additional help/practice.
5. Review or reteach the skill(s) in question to students who haven't yet mastered them. This can involve one-on-one, small-group, or whole-class instruction.
6. Repeat Steps 2–5 until all students have mastered the targeted skill(s).

How is this tool used in the classroom?

✔ To test students' command of essential skills in a fun and engaging way

The examples in this section show how the tool can be used to develop Common Core language skills (the focus of this chapter), but the You Be the Teacher framework works just as well with other skills and content areas—see Teacher Talk for ideas.

EXAMPLE 1: Primary ELA

A kindergarten teacher created the task below to test students' understanding of two capitalization rules—capitalizing the letter *I* and capitalizing the first word in a sentence (Common Core L.K.2a). Students were given four sentences and asked to correct them if needed.

> M
> my favorite toy is my airplane.
> I
> i got it for my birthday.
>
> It is fun to fly around.
> M I
> maybe i will get another plane for my next birthday.

EXAMPLE 2: Elementary social studies

A social studies teacher uses tasks like the one below to help students recognize the difference between formal and informal English (Common Core L.CCR.3) and root out language that's inappropriately informal—something she wants them to start doing in their own work.

> INSTRUCTIONS: Last year's students were asked to read about conditions on the *Mayflower* and summarize what they had learned. A portion of one student's summary is shown below. Underline *two* places where the language is too informal for the given writing task, and inconsistent with the tone of the rest of the piece. Suggest possible alternatives on the back.
>
> *Life on the Mayflower wasn't exactly super easy. The decks where the passengers lived were overly crowded and offered little privacy. Sleeping arrangements weren't particularly comfortable, either. People slept on wooden pallets or hammocks; sometimes they even slept on the floor. Keeping clean was one of the biggest challenges. There weren't any bathrooms on the ship, and no real way to bathe. From what I read, that – combined with lots of people getting seasick – caused quite a stink. Getting sick...*

EXAMPLE 3: Secondary science

A science teacher does her part to reinforce Common Core writing and language skills (W.CCR.5 and L.CCR.1–2, specifically) by having students proofread science-themed passages for grammar, punctuation, and spelling errors. (She creates the passages she gives students to correct by inserting errors into existing textbook passages or articles.) Correcting these passages (see p. 139 for an example) not only lets students practice critical literacy skills, it also engages them in reading about current topics and issues.

When it comes to food, do chimps think only of themself. According to a 2012 study published in the journal Biology Letters: the answer is yes. The goal of the study, which was performed by researchers from Queen Mary University of london was to determine whether our great-ape relatives share our sensitivity to inequity. To investigate this question, Professor Keith Jensen from Queen Marys School of Biological and Chemical Sciences and his colleagues, used an ultimatum game. In it, apes were given the option to steal different amount of food from a partner. The partners response to the theft (accept/reject the remaining food) was then noted. The result? Apes consistently stole each others...

comma not colon; themselves; ?, not period; capitalize; not needed; s

Teacher Talk

➔ This tool is extremely flexible in the sense that it can be used to develop and test a variety of different skills. In the ELA/literacy realm, you could have students review a paragraph looking for

- Vocabulary usage errors (L.CCR.6)
- Evidence/details that don't support a topic sentence or claim (W.CCR.1–2)
- Overly wordy, clunky, or redundant writing (L.CCR.3)
- Improperly formatted citations/references (W.CCR.8)
- Inconsistencies in style and tone or inappropriately formal/informal language (L.CCR.3)
- Errors pertaining to the conventions of Standard Written English (L.CCR.1–2)

Options for other content areas include having students

- Check and correct vocabulary or usage errors in a foreign language class.
- Check and correct each other's form in a physical education class (e.g., while lifting weights).
- Check and correct each other's ability to sing (or play) a song in tune in a music class.
- Check and correct problem-solving or other errors in a math class (see example below).

Instructions: Check this student's work. Mark and explain any errors.

Find the zeros: $x^2 + 6x - 16$

$x^2 + 6x - 16 = 0$

$x^2 + 6x = 16$

$x^2 + 6x + 9 = 16$ ← The student forgot to add 9 to this side of the equation.

$(x + 3)^2 = 16$

$(x + 3) = \pm\sqrt{16}$

$(x + 3) = 4, \ (x + 3) = -4$

$x = 1, \ x = -7$

➔ Pressed for time? Try "dailies": Post a single sentence (or problem) on the board at the start of each day or class period. Challenge students to find and correct the errors before class gets started.

➔ Having students find and correct errors is a great way to assess their grasp of critical skills. It also familiarizes them with common errors, rendering them less likely to make those errors themselves.

References

Amelia Earhart: The Official Website. (n.d.). *Biography.* Retrieved from http://www.ameliaearhart.com/about/bio.html

American Institutes for Research. (2013, August 26). *Smarter Balanced Assessment Consortium: Practice test scoring guide: Grade 3 performance task.* Retrieved from http://sbac.portal.airast.org/wp-content/uploads/2013/07/Grade3ELAPT.pdf

Armstrong, A., Moyer, S., & Stanton, K. (2005, September). *Learning to analyze and critically evaluate ideas, arguments, and points of view.* POD—IDEA Center Learning Notes. Retrieved from http://www.theideacenter.org/sites/default/files/Objective11.pdf

Averill, E. (1983). *The fire cat.* New York: HarperCollins. (Original work published 1960)

Blum, I. H., Koskinen, P. S., Tennant, N., Parker, E. M., Straub, M., & Curry, C. (1995). Using audiotaped books to extend classroom literacy instruction into the homes of second-language learners. *Journal of Reading Behavior, 27*(4), 535–563.

Boutz, A. L., Silver, H. F., Jackson, J. W., & Perini, M. J. (2012). *Tools for thoughtful assessment: Classroom-ready techniques for improving teaching and learning.* Ho-Ho-Kus, NJ: Thoughtful Education Press.

Buehl, D. (2009). *Classroom strategies for interactive learning* (3rd ed.). Newark, DE: International Reading Association.

Burnett, F. H. (2008). *The secret garden.* London: Penguin. (Original work published 1911)

City, E. A. (2014). Talking to learn. *Educational Leadership, 72*(3), 10–16.

Conley, D. T. (2007). The challenge of college readiness. *Educational Leadership, 64*(7), 23–29.

Connell, G. (2014, January 15). Twelve steps to creating a language-rich environment [Blog post]. Retrieved from http://www.scholastic.com/teachers/top-teaching/2014/01/12-steps-creating-language-rich-environment

Doctorow, M., Wittrock, M. C., & Marks, C. (1978). Generative processes in reading comprehension. *Journal of Educational Psychology, 70*(2), 109–118.

de Brunhoff, J. (1937). *The story of Babar: The little elephant.* New York: Random House. (Original work published 1933)

Doyle, A. C. (1976). *The original illustrated Sherlock Holmes.* Secaucus, NJ: Castle. (Original work published 1892–1893)

du Bois, W. P. (1986). *The twenty-one balloons.* New York: Penguin. (Original work published 1947)

Fischetti, M. (2007, April). Steer clear. *Scientific American, 296*(4), 96–97.

Fisher, D., & Frey, N. (2007). *Checking for understanding: Formative assessment techniques for your classroom.* Alexandria, VA: ASCD.

Fisher, D., & Frey, N. (2008). *Word wise and content rich: Five essential steps to teaching academic vocabulary (grades 7–12).* Portsmouth, NH: Heinemann.

Fisher, D., & Frey, N. (2013). *Rigorous reading: Five access points for comprehending complex texts.* Thousand Oaks, CA: Corwin Press.

Hatkoff, I., Hatkoff, C., & Kahumbu, P. (2011). Owen & Mzee: The true story of a remarkable friendship. In J. Baumann, et al. (Program authors), *Journeys: A path to balanced literacy, student eBook, level 4* (pp. 613–622). New York: Houghton Mifflin Harcourt. Retrieved from http://www-k6.thinkcentral.com

Haystead, M. W., & Marzano, R. J. (2009). *Meta-analytic synthesis of studies conducted at Marzano Research Laboratory on instructional strategies*. Englewood, CO: Marzano Research Laboratory.

Herber, H. (1970). *Teaching reading in the content areas*. Englewood Cliffs, NJ: Prentice Hall.

Hornblow, L., & Hornblow, A. (1970). *Reptiles do the strangest things*. New York: Random House.

Jacobs, H. H. (2006). *Active literacy across the curriculum: Strategies for reading, writing, speaking, and listening*. Larchmont, NY: Eye on Education.

King, Jr., M. L. (2003). Letter from Birmingham Jail. In J. M. Washington (Ed.), *I have a dream: Writings and speeches that changed the world* (pp. 83–100). New York: HarperCollins.

Koskinen, P. S., & Blum, I. H. (1986). Paired repeated reading: A classroom strategy for developing fluent reading. *The Reading Teacher, 40*(1), 70–75.

Marquette University. (2011, July 7). Writing across the curriculum: *What makes writing so important?* Retrieved from http://www.marquette.edu/wac/WhatMakesWritingSoImportant.shtml

Martin, R. (1992). *The rough-face girl*. New York: Putnam and Grosset.

Martinez, R., & Barnhill, A. (2011). Impact of MP3 players on the fluency rate of beginning readers. *The International Journal of Technology, Knowledge, and Society, 7*(2), 167–176.

Marzano, R. J. (2004). *Building background knowledge for academic achievement*. Alexandria, VA: ASCD.

Marzano, R. J. (2007). *The art and science of teaching: A comprehensive framework for effective instruction*. Alexandria, VA: ASCD.

Marzano, R. J., Pickering, D. J., & Pollock, J. E. (2001). *Classroom instruction that works: Research-based strategies for increasing student achievement*. Alexandria, VA: ASCD.

Murnane, R., Sawhill, I., & Snow, C. (2012). Literacy challenges for the twenty-first century: Introducing the issue. *The Future of Children, 22*(2), 3–15.

National Governors Association Center for Best Practices, Council of Chief State School Officers. (2010). *Common Core State Standards for English language arts and literacy in history/social studies, science, and technical subjects*. Washington, DC: Author. Retrieved from http://www.corestandards.org/ELA-Literacy

National Reading Panel. (2000). *Teaching children to read: An evidence-based assessment of the scientific research literature on reading and its implications for reading instruction. Reports of the subgroups*. Washington, DC: National Institute of Child Health and Human Development.

National Research Council. (2012). *A framework for K–12 science education: Practices, crosscutting concepts, and core ideas*. Washington, DC: The National Academies Press.

NGSS Lead States. (2013). *Next Generation Science Standards: For states, by states*. Washington, DC: The National Academies Press.

Partnership for Assessment of Readiness for College and Careers (PARCC). (2013). *Grade 11 sample items*. Retrieved from http://www.parcconline.org/sites/parcc/files/Grade11SampleItems.pdf

Pfeffer, W. (2003). Wiggling worms at work. New York: HarperCollins.

Rasinski, T. (2004). Creating fluent readers. *Educational Leadership, 61*(6), 46–51.

Read, P. P. (2002). *Alive: The story of the Andes survivors*. New York: Avon. (Original work published 1974)

Reutzel, D. R. (2006). "Hey, teacher, when you say 'fluency,' what do you mean?": Developing fluency in elementary classrooms. In T. Rasinski, C. Blachowicz, and K. Lems (Eds.), *Fluency instruction: Research-based best practices* (pp. 62–85). New York: The Guilford Press.

Santa, C. M. (1988). *Content reading including study systems: Reading, writing, and studying across the curriculum*. Dubuque, IA: Kendall/Hunt.

Schwartz, R. M., & Raphael, T. E. (1985). Concept of definition: A key to improving students' vocabulary. *The Reading Teacher, 39*(2), 198–205.

Silver, H. F. (2010). *Compare & contrast: Teaching comparative thinking to strengthen student learning (A Strategic Teacher PLC Guide)*. Alexandria, VA: ASCD.

Silver, H. F., Dewing, R. T., & Perini, M. J. (2012). *The core six: Essential strategies for achieving excellence with the Common Core*. Alexandria, VA: ASCD.

Silver, H. F., Morris, S. C., & Klein, V. (2010). *Reading for meaning: How to build students' comprehension, reasoning, and problem-solving skills (A Strategic Teacher PLC Guide)*. Alexandria, VA: ASCD.

Silver, H. F., Reilly, E. C., & Perini, M. J. (2009). *The thoughtful education guide to reading for meaning*. Thousand Oaks, CA: Corwin Press.

Silver, H. F., Strong, R. W., & Perini, M. J. (2000). *Discovering nonfiction: 25 powerful teaching strategies, grades 2–6*. Los Angeles: Canter & Associates.

Silver Strong & Associates. (2013). *The Thoughtful Classroom Teacher Effectiveness Framework (quick guide)*. Ho-ho-kus, NJ: Author. Retrieved from http://www.thoughtfulclassroom.com/PDFs/TCTEF%20Quick%20Guide_082813.pdf

Smarter Balanced Assessment Consortium. (2014, April 25). *Smarter Balanced Assessment Consortium: ELA practice test scoring guide: Grade 7*. Retrieved from http://sbac.portal.airast.org/wp-content/uploads/2013/08/G7_PracticeTest_ScoringGuide_ELA.pdf

Sprenger, M. (2013, September 18). Eleven tips on teaching Common Core critical vocabulary [Blog post]. Retrieved from http://www.edutopia.org/blog/teaching-ccss-critical-vocabulary-marilee-sprenger

Strasnick, S. (2014, March 27). Degas and Cassatt: The untold story of their artistic friendship. *ARTnews*. Retrieved from http://www.artnews.com/2014/03/27/national-gallery-show-explores-artistic-friendship-of-degas-and-cassatt/

Stewart, M. (2010). *Dolphins*. Washington, DC: National Geographic.

Thomas, E. J., & Brunsting, J. R. (2010). *Styles and strategies for teaching middle school mathematics: 21 techniques for differentiating instruction and assessment*. Thousand Oaks, CA: Corwin Press.

White, E. B. (1952). *Charlotte's web*. New York: HarperCollins.

Wormeli, R. (2005). *Summarization in any subject: 50 techniques to improve student learning*. Alexandria, VA: ASCD.

Index of Standards

The purpose of this index is to help you locate places in the book where specific Common Core ELA/Literacy Standards are mentioned. The page numbers that follow each standard include references to both anchor standards and grade-specific versions of those anchor standards. The page numbers listed for Writing Standard 1, for example, correspond to pages in the book that refer to Writing Anchor Standard 1 (W.CCR.1) or to grade-specific versions of that standard (e.g., the second-grade version of Writing Standard 1, W.2.1).

Index of Tools

A Guide to Common Core Abbreviations

Throughout this book, we use the notation system outlined in the Common Core ELA/Literacy Standards (NGA Center/CCSSO, 2010, p. 8) when abbreviating both anchor standards and grade-specific standards. The diagram below shows how this notation system works for anchor standards, using Writing Anchor Standard 3 as a model.

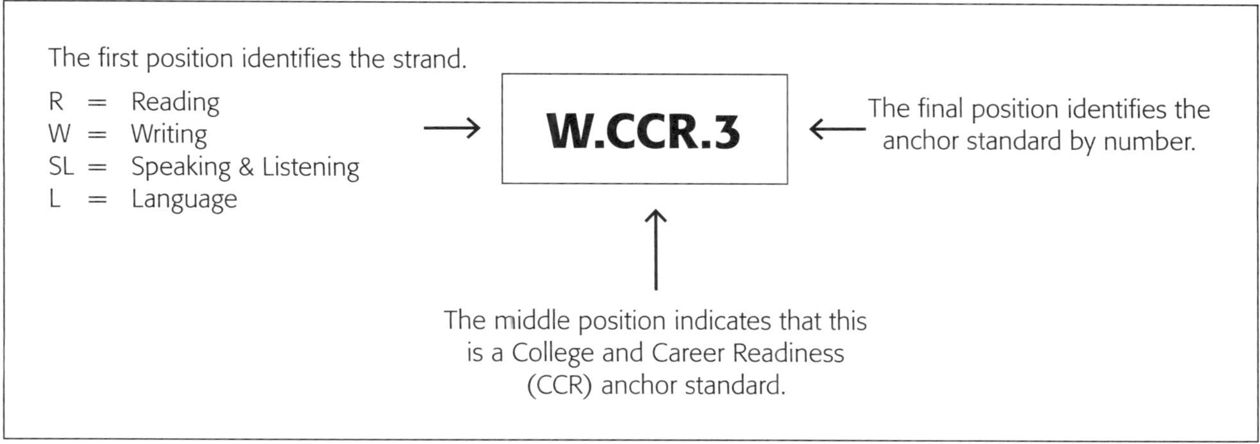

When referring to grade-specific standards, the CCR in the middle position is replaced by the appropriate grade level(s). Standard W.2.3, for example, refers to the second-grade version of Writing Standard 3.

Note that the Reading Strand contains three separate domains: Reading Literature (RL), Reading Informational Text (RI), and Reading Foundational Skills (RF). Thus, Standard RL.2.1 refers to the second-grade version of Reading Literature Standard 1.

About the Authors

Harvey F. Silver, EdD, cofounder and president of Silver Strong & Associates, has over thirty years of experience as a teacher, administrator, and consultant. He is a regular speaker at national and regional educational conferences, addressing a wide range of topics, including differentiated instruction, thoughtful assessment, school leadership, strategies for conquering the Common Core, and lesson/unit design. Dr. Silver also conducts workshops for schools, districts, and educational organizations throughout North America. He is the co-author of several educational best sellers, including *Tools for Thoughtful Assessment; Tools for Promoting Active, In-Depth Learning*; and *The Core Six*—a book of research-based strategies for addressing the Common Core State Standards. He has also collaborated with Matthew J. Perini to develop The Thoughtful Classroom Teacher Effectiveness Framework, a comprehensive teacher evaluation system that is being implemented in school districts across the country.

Abigail L. Boutz, PhD, has taught, tutored, and mentored students at the elementary through college levels, most recently at the University of California, Los Angeles, where she served as a lecturer for the Life Sciences Department, a University Field Supervisor for the Teacher Education Program, and Academic Coordinator for the Undergraduate Research Center/Center for Academic and Research Excellence. During her tenure with Silver Strong & Associates, she has designed training modules and workshop materials on classroom tools and strategies, learning styles, and instructional leadership. She has also co-authored another book in the Tools for Today's Educators series: the award-winning *Tools for Thoughtful Assessment*.

Notes